LEARN | SERVE | SUCCEED

TOOLS and TECHNIQUES for YOUTH SERVICE-LEARNING

KATE McPHERSON

SEARCH
INSTITUTE
PRESS

Learn, Serve, Succeed:
Tools and Techniques for Youth Service-Learning
Kate McPherson

Search Institute Press, Minneapolis, MN
Copyright © 2011 by Search Institute

10 9 8 7 6 5 4 3 2 1
Printed on acid-free paper in the United States of America.

Search Institute
615 First Avenue Northeast, Suite 125
Minneapolis, MN 55413
www.search-institute.org
612-376-8955 • 877-240-7251

ISBN-13: 978-1-57482-275-5

Credits
Editor: Kate Brielmaier
Book Design: Percolator
Production Supervisor: Mary Ellen Buscher

Library of Congress Cataloging-in-Publication Data
McPherson, Kate.
   Learn, serve, succeed : tools and techniques for youth service-learning / Kate McPherson.
      p. cm.
   ISBN-13: 978-1-57482-275-5 (pbk.)
   ISBN-10: 1-57482-275-6 (paperback)
   1. Service learning. 2. Community and school. 3. School improvement programs. I. Title.
LC220.5.M4 2011
371.19—dc22   2011009619

About Search Institute Press

Search Institute Press is a division of Search Institute, a nonprofit organization that offers leadership, knowledge, and resources to promote positive youth development. Our mission at Search Institute Press is to provide practical and hope-filled resources to help create a world in which all young people thrive. Our products are embedded in research, and the 40 Developmental Assets®—qualities, experiences, and relationships youth need to succeed—are a central focus of our resources. Our logo, the SIP flower, is a symbol of the thriving and healthy growth young people experience when they have an abundance of assets in their lives.

Licensing and Copyright

CONTENTS

Preface v

Introduction: Why Service-Learning Matters 1

CHAPTER 1. The Elements of Successful Service-Learning 13

CHAPTER 2. Setting Academic Goals 23

CHAPTER 3. Developing Service-Learning Partnerships 37

CHAPTER 4. Youth Voice: Engaging Students and Lowering the Dropout Rate 51

CHAPTER 5. Diversity and Cultural Competence 59

CHAPTER 6. Civic Education 65

CHAPTER 7. Planning and Preparing for Success 73

CHAPTER 8. Establishing Evidence of Learning 89

CHAPTER 9. Reflection, Demonstration, and Celebration 99

CHAPTER 10. Building and Sustaining Service-Learning Programs 111

Index 117

About the Author 119

PREFACE

My commitment to service-learning is deeply rooted in my years as a classroom teacher in an inner-city K–8 school, a public high school, a private school, and an alternative school for high school seniors. I have seen service-learning transform learning in each of these settings in unique ways.

A cross-age tutoring program gave my nonreading eighth grade boys a real reason to read, because they wanted to help "their" second graders. For many, it was the first time they had felt needed and not needy. Two of my students' reading abilities went up four grade levels in just one year.

When my U.S. history students interviewed people in our community about World War II, a human face and story made the events of history come alive. For many, their relationships with their grandparents were filled with lively conversations. The quality of their writing significantly improved when they edited and published their stories in a book that was distributed to and read by community members.

When I taught at a private school, students from my Contemporary Problems class visited the residences of people who had recently gotten off the streets. Meeting someone who had graduated from their school, had been a lawyer, and then suffered from mental illness showed them that the causes of homelessness are complex. They began to explore issues of social justice and how our country treats mental illness. Their research and writing was much more authentic as they examined the complexity of this issue.

And when my students at an alternative school chose to address an issue that mattered to them and the community, they learned how to work with public officials and media to get things done. One group worked with the city to create a walking trail so people could enjoy nature close to their town. They led the project from start to finish: surveying the park land for endangered plants, plotting and constructing a nature trail, and creating interpretive signage. Many years later these students take their children to explore along this same trail.

The magic of service-learning is how uniquely it manifests in each school community—on Bainbridge Island students researched and worked with environmentalists to remove a dam and reestablish a fish habitat. At Heritage High School students from the small-engines class partner with their peers from the AP chemistry class to convert the fat in their kitchen into biodiesel, transforming the high school into an alternative fuels magnet. And at Riverdale High School every senior leaves a personal legacy in the community through a year-long research and action project.

It is these experiences that continue to fuel my commitment to the practice of high-quality service-learning and to help teachers who want to give a solid answer to students' question, "So why are we learning this?" I hope this book will help educators answer that question for themselves as well as their students.

Special thanks to the following educators, whose strong work and thinking form the backbone of the book: Mary Stell, John Hagney, Beth Nickel, Karen Belsey, Myra Clark, MaryAnn LaZelle, Angie Robles, Angela Nusom, Nan Peterson, Santha Cassell, Kim Huseman, Barbara Yeatman, Joshua Mead, Shelley Berman, Shelley Billig, Juliet de Jesus Alejandre, Heather Pavona, Dr. Ada Grabowski, Susan Starweather, Jon Schmidt, Susie Richards, Chris Burt, and Lois Brewer. Thanks for your thoughtful work, courage, and tenacity.

The writing and thinking of the following people always push my own thinking and help the service-learning field become more impactful: Caryn Pernu, Maddy Wegner, Cathryn Berger Kaye, Susan Abravanel, Shelley Billig, Keith Thomajan, James and Pamela Toole, Gene Roehlkepartain, Keisha Edwards, Larry Fletch, Carol Kinsley, Jim Kielsmeier, and Wokie Weah.

Service-learning leaders who support the craft of service-learning: Joe Follman, Larry Bailis, Elson Nash, Joanne Henderson, Brad Lewis, Mike Brugh, Terry Pickeral, Terri Dari, Scott Richards, Jessica Paul Werner, D. D. Gass, Tony Ganger, Mac Hall, Kim Feicke, and Marta Turner. I am grateful for this community of support in the spirit of serving the field.

Thanks to everyone's willingness to respond to desperate last-minute calls for help!

And thanks to the army of community partners, teachers, researchers, youth workers, students, parents, and administrators who are nurturing this work.

Some sections of this guide were adapted with permission from *An Asset Builder's Guide to Service-Learning* by E. C. Roehlkepartain, T. Bright, B. Margolis-Rupp, and L. I. Nelson. (Minneapolis, MN: Search Institute, 2000.)

INTRODUCTION

Why Service-Learning Matters

> Donating books to second graders is **service**.
>
> Writing a story that has defined characters and a conflict is **learning**.
>
> Interviewing second graders and writing personalized stories that make them heroes in their own story as they resolve a conflict, and then giving those books to the emergent readers is **service-learning**.
>
> Sustaining this intergenerational partnership throughout the school year and supporting students as they explore the ways they can help second graders master and enjoy reading is **an asset-rich model of service-learning**.

Service-learning serves as the robust centerpiece in many classrooms and community-based programs. If done well, service-learning is an elegant instructional strategy because it simultaneously increases students' academic mastery and fosters positive youth development while addressing a real community need. It is also an instructional approach that can be used effectively in the classroom or in afterschool youth programs. And it is being used effectively with students of all ages, with varying levels of abilities, in all academic disciplines and a wide variety of youth programs.

Wetland Watchers

Every year all 500 students at Hurst Middle School lead a community effort for wetland conservation. Students master science skills as they investigate major ecosystems and recognize physical properties and organisms. Nearly 14,000 students have volunteered over 90,000 hours as part of this project since its inception during the 1997–1998 school year.

Campfire Boys and Girls Disaster Preparedness

In partnership with Camp Fire USA, a Latino youth group completed disaster preparedness training and then focused on tornado awareness after a tornado hit a neighboring town. They researched local severe weather patterns and weather preparedness and created and distributed information in both English and Spanish to youth in local afterschool programs.

Middle School Math

Students in an eighth grade remedial math class develop fun math activities that teach basic math processes to fourth and fifth graders. Each week they go to the neighboring elementary school to tutor their elementary learning buddies. Last year students' standardized test scores improved significantly. Even more important, they now see themselves as mathematicians.

Through service-learning projects, students come to see that the skills and information being taught have value in the world outside their classrooms. Service-learning naturally motivates students because learning is no longer simply about grades. Students want to do well because what they are doing is genuinely needed and valued by their community. For example:

- If a student knows the story he is writing will be read by a second grader, he has the motivation to write it well, and spell and punctuate it correctly so "his" student can read and understand it.

- If the information students will be providing to their neighbors is intended to help them during an emergency, they need to be sure the information is accurate and readable in the languages their neighbors use.

- If a student is going to teach a math process to a younger student, first she needs to be sure she fully understands and can explain the process in order to help the younger child.

Service-learning transforms the teacher-student dynamic. The teacher becomes more of a coach, helping students use academic knowledge and skills to complete tasks that have real-world consequences.

> *Now my students do more of the learning. I give them the tools, I give them the time, and I give them direction on content. In order to get the project done they come to me and say, "I don't know this, I want to learn this." They own their own learning. It is much easier to hold them to a higher level of accountability—like a job or contract—because they want to do well because "their students" are counting on them. It's been great.*
> —MARY STELL, middle school math teacher

Service-learning is rooted in the basic principles of positive youth development because it assumes that youth are resources, that they are needed and add value to the larger community. When young people engage in service-learning they provide important insights and act as a positive force in their school or community. Using service-learning as an instructional strategy is a way for adults to weave positive youth development into daily practice. As service-learning becomes commonplace, the community begins to see and value the work of young people, while young people begin to see and understand the impact of their service.

THE BENEFITS OF SERVICE-LEARNING

While it has long had a hand in connecting academic skills to the community in meaningful ways, service-learning itself is not new. What *is* new is that during the last decade, focused funding, program development, and assessment have produced a convincing body of evidence that service-learning, if done well, produces powerful benefits for students.

Academic Achievement

A review of research indicates that high-quality service-learning, because of its utilization of effective, experiential learning strategies, contributes to a range of achievement-related benefits, including improved school attendance, higher grade point averages, better preparation for the workforce, enhanced awareness and understanding of social issues, greater motivation for learning, and heightened engagement in prosocial behaviors.[1] And several studies have shown that students who participate in service-learning have scored higher than nonparticipating students in subjects such as social studies, writing, and English/language arts.[2]

Graduation Rates

Reviews of the literature have shown that service-learning is a promising strategy for dropout prevention.[3] Service-learning activities address various components or strategies identified as important to dropout prevention, such as engaging teaching and curricula, connections between school and work, adult-student relationships, communication skills, and community involvement.

A recent telephone survey of high school students showed that:

- Over 80 percent of students who participated in service-learning said they had a more positive feeling about attending high school;

- Over 75 percent of students who were currently participating in or had in the past participated in service-learning programs agreed that service-learning classes were more interesting than other classes;

- About 45 percent of students who participated in service-learning believed that service-learning classes were more worthwhile than their other classes; and

- Over 75 percent of service-learning students said that service-learning had motivated them to work hard.[4]

Reducing the Achievement Gap

A 2005 report published in *Growing to Greatness* offers evidence that service-learning may have particular educational benefits for low-income students and schools.[5]

- Involvement in service appears to contribute to narrowing the achievement gap, with low-income students who serve doing better academically than students who do not serve.

- Service seems to have a positive relation to reducing the school success gap between students from lower- and higher-income backgrounds.

- Principals in low-income schools are more likely than other principals to believe service-learning has a positive impact on students' school success.

> *You will find service-learning everywhere in our community. The community naturally comes to the schools so students can help meet unmet needs and solve problems. And when students graduate they all know we can make a difference—large or small.*
> —Dr. Ada Grabowski, former superintendent for Albion School District

Positive Youth Development

Search Institute, a nonprofit research group, has identified 40 protective factors, the Developmental Assets, that are crucial to positive youth development. They range from external supports like a caring school climate and positive family communication to internal characteristics such as school engagement and a sense of purpose.

Search Institute has done extensive research, reviewing more than 1,200 studies from major bodies of literature, including prevention, resilience, and adolescent development, to identify what young people need to thrive. Institute researchers have documented that young people who are healthy, whether they come from the poorest or the wealthiest environments and from diverse ethnic and cultural groups, have certain meaningful elements in their lives. Researchers identified eight categories that describe these elements:

- The solid presence of **support** from others;
- A feeling of **empowerment**;
- A clear understanding of **boundaries and expectations**;
- Varied opportunities for **constructive use of time**;
- A strong **commitment to learning**;
- An appreciation of **positive values**;
- Sound **social competencies**; and
- A personal sense of **positive identity**.

Moreover, research conducted by Search Institute consistently shows that the strengths described within these categories provide a solid foundation for positive development and academic success, help protect youth from engaging in risky behavior, and promote youth acting in productive ways.

Both service-learning and positive youth development share the basic premise that young people thrive when they are viewed as resources to tap rather than problems to fix, and when given authentic opportunities to do work that is genuinely needed. The table on the following page illustrates the correlation between service-learning and Developmental Assets.

New analyses of Search Institute's research on Developmental Assets also suggest that serving others may be a "gateway asset" that builds many other assets and leads to

Service-Learning Connections to the
Eight Categories of Developmental Assets

ASSET CATEGORY	DESCRIPTION	SERVICE-LEARNING CONNECTIONS
1. Support	Young people need to experience care, love, and involvement from their family, neighbors, and many others. They need organizations and institutions that provide positive, supportive environments.	Working together on service-learning projects can cement relationships of support and caring between peers and with parents and other adults.
2. Empowerment	Young people need to be valued by their community and have opportunities to contribute to others. For this to occur, they must feel safe.	As they contribute to their world, young people become experts about issues that are important to them, and are seen and see themselves as valuable resources for their organizations and communities. Careful preparation and good supervision during their service-learning efforts help them feel safe.
3. Boundaries and Expectations	Young people need to know what is expected of them and whether behaviors are "in bounds" or "out of bounds."	Boundaries and expectations are reinforced when activities include ground rules for involvement and as adults and peers become positive role models for each other.
4. Constructive Use of Time	Young people need constructive, enriching opportunities for growth through creative activities, youth programs, involvement with a center of worship or spirituality, and quality time at home.	Service-learning provides opportunities for young people to use their time to expand their minds and hearts, offer hope and support to others, and use their creativity to deal with new challenges and opportunities.
5. Commitment to Learning	Young people need to develop a lifelong commitment to education and learning.	Education linked to action can unleash a new commitment to learning as youth apply their knowledge to issues and problems and as they are exposed to questions and situations that challenge their worldview and perspectives.
6. Positive Values	Young people need to develop strong values that guide their choices.	Through service-learning, young people not only express their positive values, they also have opportunities to affirm and internalize values that are important to them.
7. Social Competencies	Young people need skills and competencies that equip them to make positive choices, to build relationships, and to succeed in life.	Many skills and social competencies are nurtured as young people plan their activities, take action, and build relationships with their peers, adults who serve with them, and service recipients.
8. Positive Identity	Young people need a strong sense of their own purpose, power, and promise.	Service-learning becomes an important catalyst for shaping positive identity as young people discover their gifts and a place in the world through their acts of service and justice.

positive outcomes, including success in school. Service experiences are part of an over-all web of assets that provide a strong foundation for healthy development.[6]

Student Achievement

Schools where successively higher proportions of students reported experiencing "re-silience assets" such as caring relationships, meaningful opportunities to participate in schools and communities (such as through service-learning), and high expectations from teachers, parents, community adults, and peers had successively higher standard-ized achievement test scores. Building Developmental Assets can be one of the strate-gies districts and communities can use to positively affect achievement. If educators and administrators make an effort to infuse positive youth development into classroom practices and curriculum and instruction, then the already apparent link between Developmental Assets and achievement can be strengthened.[7]

Work Readiness Skills

Service-learning facilitates career exploration. As students work alongside community members during their service-learning project, they often meet people who work in business, nonprofit, and civic organizations, and they can learn for themselves what different careers involve. Many key skills and competencies needed for success in col-lege and the workplace—such as problem-solving, critical thinking and reasoning, self-management, communication skills, conflict resolution, and cultural competen-cies—are an integral part of service-learning experiences. Service-learning can also help students develop career plans that are personally satisfying and serve the community.

Civic Engagement

Through service-learning experiences students can learn about social and political structures, discover disparities and injustices, and realize that they can have an impact on community decisions and conditions. As a result, students typically develop a sense of civic awareness and responsibility.

- Compared to their peers, young adults who participated in service-learning were more likely to discuss politics or community issues, more politically and socially connected to their communities, both as leaders and role models, and more active members of society.[8]

- Students involved in service-learning had higher scores of overall school enjoy-ment than comparison group peers and were significantly more likely to report intending to vote than comparison students.[9]

WHO CAN USE THIS BOOK

This guide is designed to help you develop strategies for implementing service-learning so that it fits your school or community context. Because it emphasizes how class-room teachers and community educators can effectively use service-learning to teach academic skills and content, it will introduce the K–12 Service-Learning Standards for

Benefits of Asset-Based Service-Learning

There are many good, general reasons for engaging youth in asset-based service-learning. Here are a few examples of the benefits:

For the Participating Young People

- Engaging in service to others can build many of the Developmental Assets, which provide a foundation for healthy development and choices.

- Service-learning changes others' perceptions of young people from problems to resources.

- It helps them learn academic skills through active, hands-on experiences and develops their leadership potential.

- It connects them with caring and responsible adults and peers.

- It widens and diversifies their worldview to include others who may not be a part of their everyday lives.

For the Educator

- Service-learning is something new and refreshing that can add variety to an educator's routine.

- It gets teachers and learners out of the classroom and into the community.

- It fosters closer connections between teachers or youth workers and the young people they work with.

- Service-learning improves academic outcomes.

For the Sponsoring Organization

- Service-learning provides a potentially powerful strategy for fulfilling their mission, whether it's learning (schools), personal development (youth organizations), or growth in faith (religious organizations).

- It keeps young people engaged, connected, motivated, and excited about participation in learning and other activities.

- It provides a service to the community and those in need.

- It can energize the whole organization as young people's passion, commitment, and enthusiasm rub off on other people.

For the Recipients of Service

- Service-learning meets real needs.

- It provides them an opportunity to build relationships with people of all ages.

- It can offer new hope, encouragement, and confidence in the goodwill of others.

For the Larger Community

- Young people bring new energy, capabilities, and creative ideas for building community and addressing specific needs.

- Service-learning cultivates a new generation of caring and experienced activists and volunteers.

- Young people become valuable resources to the community.

Quality Practice, and some practical tools that can help you enhance the success of your projects. It will focus on the practical application of these standards in a variety of settings. It is designed to support:

- **Teachers or youth leaders** who are already implementing service-learning to explore ways to deepen or enrich their practice and explore ways to celebrate and sustain their work.

- **Service-learning coordinators** who plan to deepen or broaden practice in their school or district through professional development for adult leaders or establishing community partners.

- **Community educators** who are strengthening the academic impact of their service-learning programs.

- **Staff development or curriculum directors** who are integrating service-learning into instructional frameworks their district is using to improve student mastery and engagement.

- **District or organizational leaders** who plan to weave service-learning into the core fabric of their district mission.

The primary emphasis of this book will be school-based service-learning, but you'll also find examples of youth-serving and nonprofit organizations that are effectively using this instructional strategy to increase academic learning and community impacts. And you will find examples of a few schools, districts, and organizations that have made service-learning a central strategy for academic and youth development.

MORE ABOUT THE 40 DEVELOPMENTAL ASSETS

Search Institute identified 40 components of youth development known as *Developmental Assets*. The data consistently show that the power of assets is cumulative: The more assets young people experience, the more apt they are to succeed in school and lead positive lives, and the less likely they are to participate in high-risk behaviors such as drug use, violence, and early sexual activity.

NOTES

1. A. Furco, "The role of service-learning in enhancing student achievement," presentation given at the National Center for Learning and Citizenship Board Meeting, Santa Barbara, CA, 2007.
2. N. Kraft and J. Wheeler, "Service-learning and resilience in disaffected youth: A research study," in S. H. Billig and J. Eyler, eds., *Advances in service-learning research: Vol. 3. Deconstructing service-learning: Research exploring context, participation, and impacts*, Greenwich, CT: Information Age, 2003, 213–238; A. Furco and B. Granicher, *California service-learning district partnerships: Statewide summary report of local evaluations 2005–2006*, Sacramento, CA: California Department of Education, 2007.
3. J. Bridgeland, J. DiIulio Jr., and S. Wulsin, report by Civic Enterprises in association with Peter D. Hart Research Associates for the National Conference on Citizenship, 2008.
4. "Fact Sheets: Dropout Prevention and Service-Learning," RMC Research Corporation, 2008, accessed at www.servicelearning.org/instant_info/fact_sheets/k-12_facts/dropout_prevention.

5. J. Kielsmeier, M. Neal, and A. Crossley, *Growing to Greatness 2006: The State of Service-Learning Project*, St. Paul, MN: National Youth Leadership Council, 2007.

6. P. C. Scales and E. C. Roehlkepartain, "Can service-learning help reduce the achievement gap?" in J. Kielsmeier and M. Neal, eds., *Growing to Greatness 2005: The State of Service-Learning in the United States,* St. Paul, MN: National Youth Leadership Council, 2006.

7. P. C. Scales, et al., "The role of developmental assets in predicting academic achievement: A longitudinal study," *Journal of Adolescence* 29 (2006): 691–708.

8. D. Markow, et al., "The National Survey on Service-Learning and Transitioning to Adulthood," St. Paul, MN: National Youth Leadership Council and Harris Interactive, 2005.

9. S. H. Billig, S. Root, and D. Jesse, "The relationship between quality indicators of service-learning and student outcomes: Testing professional wisdom," in S. Root, J. Callahan, and S. H. Billig, eds., *Advances in service-learning research: Vol. 5 Improving service-learning practice: research on models to enhance impacts,* Greenwich, CT; Information Age, 2005: 97–115.

The Framework of 40 Developmental Assets® for Adolescents

Search Institute has identified the following building blocks of healthy development that help young people grow up healthy, caring, and responsible.

EXTERNAL ASSETS

Support

1. *Family Support*—Family life provides high levels of love and support.

2. *Positive Family Communication*—Young person and her or his parent(s) communicate positively, and young person is willing to seek advice and counsel from parent(s).

3. *Other Adult Relationships*—Young person receives support from three or more nonparent adults.

4. *Caring Neighborhood*—Young person experiences caring neighbors.

5. *Caring School Climate*—School provides a caring, encouraging environment.

6. *Parent Involvement in Schooling*—Parent(s) are actively involved in helping young person succeed in school.

Empowerment

7. *Community Values Youth*—Young person perceives that adults in the community value youth.

8. *Youth as Resources*—Young people are given useful roles in the community.

9. *Service to Others*—Young person serves in the community one hour or more per week.

10. *Safety*—Young person feels safe at home, at school, and in the neighborhood.

Boundaries and Expectations

11. *Family Boundaries*—Family has clear rules and consequences and monitors the young person's whereabouts.

12. *School Boundaries*—School provides clear rules and consequences.

13. *Neighborhood Boundaries*—Neighbors take responsibility for monitoring young people's behavior.

14. *Adult Role Models*—Parent(s) and other adults model positive, responsible behavior.

15. *Positive Peer Influence*—Young person's best friends model responsible behavior.

16. *High Expectations*—Both parent(s) and teachers encourage the young person to do well.

Constructive Use of Time

17. *Creative Activities*—Young person spends three or more hours per week in lessons or practice in music, theater, or other arts.

18. *Youth Programs*—Young person spends three or more hours per week in sports, clubs, or organizations at school and/or in the community.

19. *Religious Community*—Young person spends one or more hours per week in activities in a religious institution.

20. *Time at Home*—Young person is out with friends "with nothing special to do" two or fewer nights per week.

INTERNAL ASSETS

Commitment to Learning

21. *Achievement Motivation*—Young person is motivated to do well in school.

22. *School Engagement*—Young person is actively engaged in learning.

23. *Homework*—Young person reports doing at least one hour of homework every school day.

24. *Bonding to School*—Young person cares about her or his school.

25. *Reading for Pleasure*—Young person reads for pleasure three or more hours per week.

Positive Values

26. *Caring*—Young person places high value on helping other people.

27. *Equality and Social Justice*—Young person places high value on promoting equality and reducing hunger and poverty.

28. *Integrity*—Young person acts on convictions and stands up for her or his beliefs.

29. *Honesty*—Young person "tells the truth even when it is not easy."

30. *Responsibility*—Young person accepts and takes personal responsibility.

31. *Restraint*—Young person believes it is important not to be sexually active or to use alcohol or other drugs.

Social Competencies

32. *Planning and Decision Making*—Young person knows how to plan ahead and make choices.

33. *Interpersonal Competence*—Young person has empathy, sensitivity, and friendship skills.

34. *Cultural Competence*—Young person has knowledge of and comfort with people of different cultural/racial/ethnic backgrounds.

35. *Resistance Skills*—Young person can resist negative peer pressure and dangerous situations.

36. *Peaceful Conflict Resolution*—Young person seeks to resolve conflict nonviolently.

Positive Identity

37. *Personal Power*—Young person feels he or she has control over "things that happen to me."

38. *Self-Esteem*—Young person reports having a high self-esteem.

39. *Sense of Purpose*—Young person reports that "my life has a purpose."

40. *Positive View of Personal Future*—Young person is optimistic about her or his personal future.

The Power of Assets

On one level, the 40 Developmental Assets® represent common wisdom about the kinds of positive experiences and characteristics that young people need and deserve. But their value extends further. Surveys of more than 2 million young people in grades 6–12 have shown that assets are powerful influences on adolescent behavior. (The numbers below reflect 2003 data from 148,189 young people in 202 communities.) Regardless of the gender, ethnic heritage, economic situation, or geographic location of the youth surveyed, these assets both promote positive behaviors and attitudes and help protect young people from many different problem behaviors.

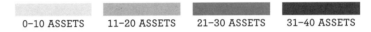

0–10 ASSETS   11–20 ASSETS   21–30 ASSETS   31–40 ASSETS

PROMOTING POSITIVE BEHAVIORS AND ATTITUDES

Search Institute research shows that the more assets students report having, the more likely they are to report the following patterns of thriving behavior:

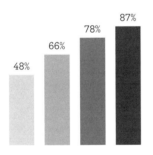

Exhibits Leadership
Has been a leader of an organization or group in the past 12 months.

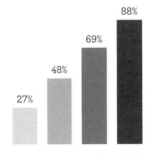

Maintains Good Health
Takes good care of body (such as eating foods that are healthy and exercising regularly).

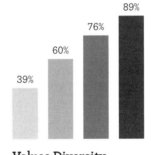

Values Diversity
Thinks it is important to get to know people of other racial/ethnic groups.

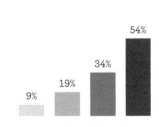

Succeeds in School
Gets mostly A's on report card (an admittedly high standard).

PROTECTING YOUTH FROM HIGH-RISK BEHAVIORS

Assets not only promote positive behaviors, they also protect young people. The more assets a young person has, the less likely she is to make harmful or unhealthy choices.

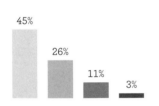

Illicit Drug Use
Used illicit drugs (marijuana, cocaine, LSD, heroin, or amphetamines) three or more times in the past 12 months.

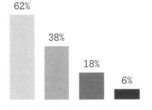

Problem Alcohol Use
Has used alcohol three or more times in the past 30 days or got drunk once or more in the past two weeks.

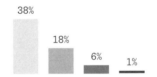

Violence
Has engaged in three or more acts of fighting, hitting, injuring a person, carrying a weapon, or threatening physical harm in the past 12 months.

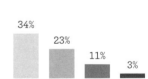

Sexual Activity
Has had sexual intercourse three or more times in her or his lifetime.

The Elements of Successful Service-Learning

Caryn Pernu, National Youth Leadership Council, lead writer

Students gain a lot from successful service-learning. The academic, personal, and social skills service-learning fosters are important for young people who want to leave school ready for the workplace or for higher education.

But not all service-learning has the level of quality that will encourage these beneficial outcomes. Fortunately, research and the experience of seasoned service-learning educators has been used to develop a set of standards for how to do service-learning well.

The K–12 Service-Learning Standards for Quality Practice were developed by National Youth Leadership Council in partnership with RMC Research in Denver and a variety of organizations and educators from across the United States. Years of work went into creating a set of evidence-based standards that can guide teachers in providing students with high-quality opportunities for learning.

For a downloadable version of the K–12 Service-Learning Standards for Quality Practice and their corresponding indicators, as well as background research that supports the standards and a description of the standards-setting process, visit nylc.org/standards.

K–12 SERVICE-LEARNING STANDARDS FOR QUALITY PRACTICE

The following standards offer teachers guidance on implementing service-learning in their classrooms and are critical to the success of service-learning projects. While not every standard can be included at a high level in each project you might tackle, it's important to understand the elements and what they bring to the experience.

1. Meaningful Service
2. Link to Curriculum
3. Reflection
4. Diversity

5. Youth Voice
6. Partnerships
7. Progress Monitoring
8. Duration and Intensity

Meaningful Service

Service-learning actively engages participants in meaningful and personally relevant service activities. Service-learning

- provides experiences appropriate to participant ages and developmental abilities;
- addresses issues that are personally relevant to the participants;
- provides participants with interesting and engaging service activities;
- encourages participants to understand their service experiences in the context of the underlying societal issues being addressed; and
- leads to attainable and visible outcomes that are valued by those being served.

To meet this standard, students work on issues that are real concerns in their community and that matter both to them and to those they serve. Young people help identify the community need their service will address and collaborate with those they will serve to ensure that the proposed solution to the problem is meaningful and desired. One common barrier to meaningful service develops when the proposed recipients of the service aren't consulted to be sure that they would value the students' proposed solution to an identified problem. An understanding of the community is key to implementing any project.

Link to Curriculum

Service-learning is intentionally used as an instructional strategy to meet learning goals and/or content standards. Service-learning

- has clearly articulated learning goals;
- is aligned with the academic and/or youth program curriculum;
- helps participants learn how to transfer knowledge and skills from one setting to another; and
- is formally recognized in school board policies and student records.

This standard requires a project's learning goals to be articulated clearly, not only so that everyone involved—teachers, students, and community partners—understands and supports the goals but also so that the service can be aligned with the learning throughout the project. When the academic goals are clear and the service has been identified, it becomes easier for students to practice the skills and incorporate the knowledge they need to demonstrate.

Teachers find a variety of entry points into the learning goals. Sometimes a community need generates ideas for projects, other times the learning goals provide a context that needs to be taken into consideration. Often, the work of linking classroom goals to the action plan proceeds in several directions at once. (See page 29 for a more detailed discussion of entry points.)

Reflection

Service-learning incorporates multiple challenging reflection activities that are on-going and that prompt deep thinking and analysis about oneself and one's relationship to society. Service-learning reflection

- includes a variety of verbal, written, artistic, and nonverbal activities to demonstrate understanding and changes in participants' knowledge, skills, and/or attitudes;
- occurs before, during, and after the service experience;
- prompts participants to think deeply about complex community problems and alternative solutions;
- encourages participants to examine their preconceptions and assumptions in order to explore and understand their roles and responsibilities as citizens; and
- encourages participants to examine a variety of social and civic issues related to their service-learning experience.

Reflection is one of the core components of service-learning. It's not just a backward-looking analysis of a project, however, but something that's intentionally worked in at every stage of learning—before, during, and after the service experience. This helps students—and teachers and community partners—understand the connection between what they're learning and the action they're taking as well as their personal assumptions about their service and viewpoints of the issues involved. As the project continues, reflection opportunities prompt participants to examine whether their knowledge has expanded or their views and assumptions have changed as a result of the experience. When this standard is being met, students also explore complex local and global problems and potential solutions, and consider their roles and responsibilities in realizing these solutions.

Diversity

Service-learning promotes understanding of diversity and mutual respect among all participants. Service-learning

- helps participants identify and analyze different points of view to gain an understanding of multiple perspectives;
- helps participants develop interpersonal skills in conflict resolution and group decision-making;
- helps participants actively seek to understand and value the diverse backgrounds and perspectives of those offering and receiving service; and
- encourages participants to recognize and overcome stereotypes.

Through partnering, collaborating, and working with various individuals and groups, students engaged in service-learning come into contact with others very different from themselves. They may cross any number of dividing lines—age, gender, race, cultural background, economic status, politics. Whether those lines fade or grow into barriers depends on how openly the participants learn to focus on the ultimate goals—learning and service—instead of on personal biases or preconceptions. This links directly to reflection, because it requires everyone to examine and openly deal with perceived boundaries and stereotypes. In most cases, when honest openness is maintained, the boundaries disappear and lines of connection form instead.

Participants learn to value each other, and if they do not come to share the same viewpoints, they at least understand and respect them. The process of working with and for others who are different from themselves triggers the development of interpersonal skills. In service-learning, students learn how to work within a group and solve problems as they arise.

Youth Voice

Service-learning provides youth with a strong voice in planning, implementing, and evaluating service-learning experiences with guidance from adults. Service-learning

- engages youth in generating ideas during the planning, implementation, and evaluation processes;
- involves youth in the decision-making process throughout the service-learning experiences;
- involves youth and adults in creating an environment that supports trust and open expression of ideas;
- promotes acquisition of knowledge and skills to enhance youth leadership and decision-making; and
- involves youth in evaluating the quality and effectiveness of the service-learning experience.

Service-learning is often the one time within the school day that students have the opportunity to have a real voice in what they are trying to accomplish. With service-learning, students are engaged in generating ideas, expressing opinions, sharing insights, discussing options, evaluating processes, and making decisions.

When students trust that their voices will be heard—when they are confident that their ideas will be considered and not overridden or arbitrarily turned down—it makes them *want* to do the work. They begin to see themselves as capable of making a contribution and respected for it. Youth voice cultivates not only useful action but also responsibility, self-respect, respect for others, and a sense of commitment.

Partnerships

Service-learning partnerships are collaborative, mutually beneficial, and address community needs. Service-learning partnerships

- involve a variety of partners, including youth, educators, families, community members, community-based organizations, and/or businesses;
- are characterized by frequent and regular communication to keep all partners well informed about activities and progress;

- collaborate to establish a shared vision and set common goals to address community needs;

- collaboratively develop and implement action plans to meet specified goals; and

- share knowledge and understanding of school and community assets and needs, and view each other as valued resources.

Partnerships are simultaneously one of the most rewarding and challenging aspects for many teachers doing service-learning. Working collaboratively, as you are asking your students to do when they take part in a service-learning project, can be difficult for many teachers who are used to going it alone in the classroom. But the partnerships developed through service-learning and working with people from the community eventually bring far more to the classroom than the effort it takes to forge the relationships.

Potential partners include youth, other educators, families, community members, community-based organizations, businesses, government, and faith-based organizations.

Progress Monitoring

Service-learning engages participants in an ongoing process to assess the quality of implementation and progress toward meeting specified goals, and uses results for improvement and sustainability. Service-learning participants

- collect evidence of progress toward meeting specific service goals and learning outcomes from multiple sources throughout the service-learning experience;

- collect evidence of the quality of service-learning implementation from multiple sources throughout the service-learning experience;

- use evidence to improve service-learning experiences; and

- communicate evidence of progress toward goals and outcomes with the broader community, including policy-makers and education leaders, to deepen service-learning understanding and ensure that high-quality practices are sustained.

As schools today become more data-driven, the idea of monitoring the progress of a service-learning project is likely not going to be an unfamiliar concept to most teachers. It involves collecting evidence, using that evidence, and then communicating that evidence to others at each stage of the service-learning experience.

While you will be monitoring student learning and progress toward the service goals, everyone who participates in the project should also play a role in monitoring its success.

Monitoring the work as it unfolds requires everyone's close attention to problems as they arise, to academic goals and service goals, and to the needs of all participants. Ideally, by the end of the work, project monitoring has created a record of all the issues that have arisen and how well they have been addressed. It is a record derived from constant communication and in-the-moment adjustments and improvements.

Duration and Intensity

Service-learning has sufficient duration and intensity to address community needs and meet specified outcomes. Service-learning

- includes the processes of investigating community needs, preparing for service, action, reflection, demonstration of learning and impacts, and celebration;
- is conducted during concentrated blocks of time across a period of several weeks or months; and
- provides enough time to address identified community needs and achieve learning outcomes.

Recent research has shown that projects must be of sufficient duration to have an impact on students.[1] It needs to include preparation, action, reflection, and demonstration of results. Fewer hours simply do not give students enough time to grapple with difficult issues or to have a deep enough experience to make the learning endure. This makes sense in the context of good teaching and learning and knowledge of a coherent curriculum that focuses on important ideas or skills.

THE SERVICE-LEARNING CYCLE

Service-learning is an intentional process that requires attention to learning goals, community needs, and student interest. Teachers doing service-learning juggle many ideas at once as they guide their students through service-learning experiences.

Many models have been developed over the years to help teachers and students organize, act, and reflect on their service-learning experiences. NYLC's Service-Learning Cycle (see pages 19–20) is one such model that has proven successful in guiding participants to create high-quality learning through service.

The service-learning cycle is not necessarily a linear process where you must progress through the steps in order. Sometimes you'll accomplish the steps simultaneously. Sometimes you will start with the community need rather than the academic environment you're working within. But you'll always have planning and research activities that need to be done before beginning the project. You'll always have to take the time to reflect before, during, and after the service component. And you'll always have other activities to accomplish following the service activity.

Pre-Service

1. **Identify the academic environment.** Educators lay the groundwork for effective service-learning by outlining their academic obligations, their goals for their students, and the resources they have available. This planning sets the stage to describe the overarching academic goals students will achieve in their service-learning experience.

2. **Identify genuine needs.** Sometimes a community member or organization may come to you with a need identified. Other times students will go through a specific process such as community mapping or a media scan to explore their communities

The
Service-Learning Cycle

Service-learning is best thought of as a cycle, where each step in the process leads to the next. As the diagram of the Service-Learning Cycle illustrates, the process doesn't end with the completion of the service activity. A project may be completed, but service-learning is a transformational process, where young people, practitioners, and communities continue to grow.

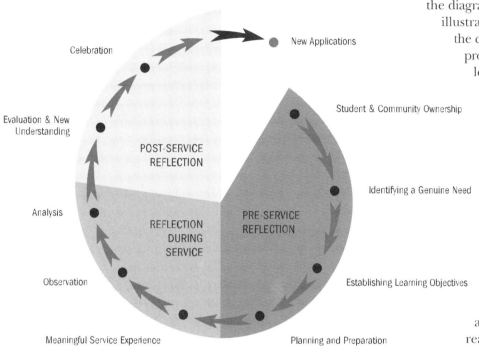

Celebration

New Applications

Evaluation & New Understanding

Student & Community Ownership

POST-SERVICE REFLECTION

Identifying a Genuine Need

Analysis

REFLECTION DURING SERVICE

PRE-SERVICE REFLECTION

Observation

Establishing Learning Objectives

Meaningful Service Experience

Planning and Preparation

WHAT? • SO WHAT? • NOW WHAT?

Illustration copyright ©2005 by NYLC and Compass Institute. All Rights Reserved.

Every part of the cycle is rich with learning and growth opportunities, many of them happening as young people are guided through the process of identifying, planning, and carrying out service activities. It's important for practitioners to recognize the learning potential in each phase of the process and get students reflecting so that real learning takes place.

With each step in a service-learning project, discussing three deceptively simple questions with the participants helps everyone understand what they've accomplished, learned, and need to do next:

What

What has happened? Take stock of what participants did, saw, and felt. Get their initial observations of what has happened.

So What?

What's the importance of all this? Discuss what participants are thinking and feeling about the experience. Ask them what they've learned and how things have changed.

Now What?

What should we do next? It's time to decide how best to channel this new understanding into continued action and transformation.

See next page for a detailed explanation of the cycle.

National Youth Leadership Council
1667 Snelling Avenue North
Suite D300
Saint Paul, MN 55108

Pre-Service

Reflection
Students get the most out of the service experience when they carefully examine their prior knowledge of and opinions on issues raised by the project.

Student & Community Ownership
The project belongs to the participants. Young people and community members should work together to identify community needs, plan service activities, and evaluate the impact of the project.

Identifying a Genuine Need
A "genuine need" is one that's important to the young people *and* the community. To identify the need, young people must recognize relevant issues, assess resources, and seek out the thoughts and concerns of those being served.

Establishing Learning Objectives
Clear learning objectives distinguish *service-learning* from *community service*. When students make the connections between their service activities and studies, it deepens their understanding of the curricular material, how it's used, and why it's important.

Planning & Preparation
No project succeeds without careful planning and preparation, and service-learning projects are no exception. Be sure to assess needs, collect all relevant information, engage in the necessary training, build vital partnerships, and develop an action plan.

During Service

Reflection
This is a chance to discover where young people are in the learning process, and give them a chance to voice concerns and share feelings.

Meaningful Service Experience
By investing themselves fully in service activities that address genuine community needs, young people find meaning in the project and grow to understand its value.

Observation
To truly understand the impact of the service, young people should take time to observe the impact of the project on different participants. This process may involve exchanging ideas with peers and community partners, looking at the implications of cultural and diversity issues, or viewing the project in civic or political terms.

Analysis
As young people use their observations to recognize the significance of the service experience, they assess their own learning and the impact of the project on the community being served.

Post-Service

Reflection
Young people take time to assess the meaning of the service experience; integrate their new understanding; and propose further action, projects, or enhancements to the current project.

Evaluation & New Understanding
Evaluating their learning and the results of the project allows young people to discover new and different perceptions of themselves and the world around them.

Celebration
All involved should enjoy the fruits of their labor and respect the accomplishments of other participants. This reinforces the positive achievements, sense of accomplishment, and personal growth attained through the service-learning experience.

New Applications
The project may be completed, but participants continue to use their new knowledge and skills to make decisions, solve problems, and grow as caring, contributing members of their communities.

www.nylc.org

National Youth Leadership Council
1667 Snelling Avenue North
Suite D300
Saint Paul, MN 55108

and learn about relevant issues. You and your students will assess resources and discover what's important to the class and the community before developing a project.

3. **Establish learning objectives.** Once you have a specific framework for the community need and academic goals the experience will address, you can ask, "What are the learning outcomes that students can achieve in addressing the needs they identified?" Link your specific academic objectives to the planned service and identify the actions needed, and communicate them clearly with the students so they know what's expected of them.

4. **Develop ownership.** With strong projects, service-learning coordinators, classroom teachers, students, and community partners all develop a sense of engagement, investment, and ownership in the work that's being done. All these participants evaluate what they bring to the experience and set goals, laying a sustainable foundation on which to build.

5. **Plan and prepare.** Before beginning the service activity, you and your students will collect relevant information, develop the project plan, engage in the necessary training, build vital partnerships, and gather the necessary resources to implement student ideas about how to improve their communities.

Service

6. **Conduct meaningful service.** Although the service activity is at the heart of service-learning, it's most often the shortest part of the cycle. Young people participate in interesting and engaging service activities that meet classroom objectives while addressing a genuine need.

Post-Service

7. **Evaluate the experience.** Service-learning participants observe the effects of their project on different participants, and exchange ideas with peers and community partners. Students analyze these observations to better understand the significance of their service experience, comparing their prior knowledge with new understandings of academic content, their own skills and contributions, and the project's impact on the community. You and your students evaluate how they met academic objectives and service goals.

8. **Demonstrate new understanding.** Now that they've learned something through their experience, students can reach out to other potential community partners— school boards, parent-teacher organizations, media outlets, legislative bodies— to present their findings, share community outcomes, and consider possible next steps. This is another opportunity for students to practice the new skills and apply the knowledge they've gained through the experience.

9. **Go deeper.** Educators, students, and other participants continue to use their new knowledge and skills to make decisions, solve problems, and grow as engaged learners and contributing members of the community. Students come to understand root issues underlying community needs.

RESOURCES

High Quality Instruction That Transforms: A Guide to Implementing Quality Academic Service-Learning by Teri Dary, Betsy Prueter, Jane Grinde, Richard Grobschmidt, and Tony Evers. Wisconsin Department of Public Instruction, 2010. Bringing together resources from RMC Research, the National Service-Learning Clearinghouse, and input from educators, this guide provides the step-by-step process to creating a high-quality service-learning experience as well as resources and teacher and student worksheets. At dpi.wi.gov/fscp/pdf/sl-implementationguide.pdf.

Service-Learning in Afterschool Programs: Resources for Afterschool Educators by Youth Service California, 2006. Created by and for afterschool educators, this guide features tried-and-true tools and examples from K–12 afterschool programs, the seven elements of high-quality service-learning in afterschool programs, and five easy steps to implementing service-learning in afterschool programs. Available at the National Service Learning Clearinghouse, servicelearning.org.

The **National Youth Leadership Council** website is filled with clear resources that can help teachers apply the standards to their service-learning practice. There are tip sheets for each standard, and schools can join a network of educators through the Generator School Network. At nylc.org.

The **National Service Learning Clearinghouse** is filled with a rich variety of fact sheets, research studies, and curriculum examples. At servicelearning.org.

Inspired to Serve provides resources and ideas that will help strengthen faith-based and interfaith service and service-learning. At inspiredtoserve.org

The Lift is an online tool that brings the K–12 Service Learning Standards for High Quality Practice to life through video clips and resources. At gsn.nylc.org/learn/lift.

Youth Service America's *Semester of Service* **manual** provides ways to put the K–12 Service-Learning Standards into practice. At ysa.org/resources.

NOTE

1. S. H. Billig, S. Root, and D. Jesse, "The relationship between quality indicators of service-learning and student outcomes: Testing professional wisdom," in S. Root, J. Callahan, and S. H. Billig, eds., *Advances in service-learning research: Vol.5. Improving service-learning practice: research on models to enhance impacts,* Greenwich, CT; Information Age, 2005: 97–115; P. C. Scales and E. C. Roehlkepartain, "Can service-learning help reduce the achievement gap?" in J. Kielsmeier and M. Neal, eds., *Growing to Greatness 2005: The State of Service-Learning Project,* St. Paul, MN: National Youth Leadership Council, 2006.

Setting Academic Goals

The first step in planning your service-learning project is to determine the program purpose and student learning goals. In other words, you want to make sure the service-learning project fits into your school or program's academic requirements and that you understand the time, resources, and staffing constraints that you must work within.

Given the increased accountability, it is more important than ever that students master and demonstrate specific academic skills. Service-learning curriculum also needs to be intellectually rigorous in order for it to help prepare students for college, careers, and citizenship.

The specific goals you set will vary widely based on the age of the young people involved, your school's curricular focus, and the specific content areas you teach. Now is also the time to begin to consider how you'll assess the success of the project, both in terms of student learning outcomes and the service outcomes.

The following natural starting points can help teachers determine the best focus for an academically rigorous service-learning curriculum.

DEMONSTRATE MASTERY

Could your students take a process they've learned in class and use it to solve a problem?

Biodiesel Project

Students in the small-engines class and the AP chemistry class at Heritage High School are working together to explore how they can effectively convert the fat from their kitchen into biodiesel. They need the understanding of engine mechanics and chemistry to produce a

Generating Service-Learning Projects

Good questions can help you and your students brainstorm service-learning projects that apply content learning to authentic community needs. They will help students identify how the lessons they are learning can:

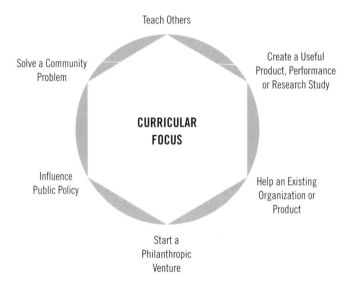

Asking the following questions can help you design a service-learning project that is aligned with both a real community need and academic learning in your specific content area(s).

Teach Others
Could your students teach what they have learned to an audience beyond the classroom?

Create a Product, Performance, or Research Study
Could your students' efforts be shaped into a product, performance, or research study that would benefit the community?

Solve a Community Problem
What are important concerns in the school or the community? How can students use their skills and knowledge to address a community need?

Influence Public Policy
Could students use what they have learned to advocate for a change in policy?

Help an Existing Organization
Could students provide direct assistance to a nonprofit or civic organization?

Start a Philanthropic Venture
Could you write a grant or raise money to fund a project or social entrepreneurial venture?

clarity of biodiesel that can eventually be used to fuel school buses in a more environmentally friendly way. Students are working on an authentic problem that demands rigorous analysis, and they often speak to the public about the results of their work and what they are learning about quality scientific research and emerging fields in alternative fuels and engine design.

ACADEMIC NEED

Are your students struggling to learn something?

Science Vertical Teaming Project PHOTO

Sophomore science teachers at Heritage High School noted that students were not doing well on the state science assessment tests. An analysis of the test results revealed that students were not able to identify various elements on the scientific process, often confused dependent and independent variables, and were not able to distinguish whether or not they had collected scientifically valid evidence. The teachers' solution was to pair their students with fourth graders to help them design and complete a science experiment that included all the elements of an effective science experiment and then host the science fair at their school. The sophomores were expected to judge the quality of other students' projects, so they had to have a clear understanding of scientific process. Both the high schoolers' and elementary students' scores on their state assessments improved.

TEACH OTHERS

Could your students teach what they are learning to an audience beyond the classroom?

Cross-Age Tutoring

Staff at Spokane's Lewis and Clark High School saw the need for interventions on behalf of students who were not reading at grade level. They created the Peer Assisted Learning System (PALS), which trained high school juniors and seniors in corrective reading. Tutors typically worked with at-risk high school students, though some were placed at elementary and middle schools. PALS tutors learned decoding, comprehension, assessment, and data collection, and some even earned Running Start college credit in applied psychology. Most tutored students gained nine months of reading skills in four months of class.

CREATE A PRODUCT, STUDY, OR PERFORMANCE

Could your students' efforts be shaped into a product or performance for an audience beyond the classroom?

Research: Human Genome Project

For several years, students in hundreds of high schools worked on the Human Genome Project, a worldwide effort to create a library of DNA codes. Biology students studied DNA synthesis and DNA sequencing, learning how to put a gene inside bacteria and how to get the bacteria to express that gene. They collected and validated data and then submitted their findings to the National Institutes of Health.

Performance: "Bang, Bang, You're Dead"

"Bang, Bang, You're Dead" is a fictional drama that's an all-too-real reminder of school shootings across the United States. The play takes place in the head of Josh, an angry high school freshman who has killed five classmates. The five dead students come to visit him and get him to understand that when he killed them, he also ended his own life. "Bang, Bang, You're Dead" is now performed in schools and community forums where people are concerned about youth violence. Actors, other youth, or teachers used guiding questions to lead discussions that brought feelings, awareness, and solutions to the forefront.

SOLVE A COMMUNITY PROBLEM

What are important concerns in the school or the community?

Generations

Middle school students were allowed to go in one of three directions with the generations theme: working with the older generation, working with the younger generation, or leaving a legacy for future generations to enjoy. Some chose child care, some chose health care for the elderly, and some chose to work in conservation, ecology, or waste management. The weekly two-hour stint of service in these areas was a centerpiece of the Generations unit, but it was only one part. Students were asked to examine the historical context of their chosen service, and, based on their experience and research, make recommendations for the future. They also worked to formulate public policies that would best address the needs they observed in their communities.

HELP AN EXISTING ORGANIZATION

Could students provide direct assistance to a nonprofit or civic organization?

Public Service Announcement Film Festival

Teams of Clover Park High School students interviewed representatives from local nonprofits, and, based on the information they gathered, developed a Public Service Announcement each organization could use to tell its story and recruit support. The school then sponsored a PSA film festival and nonprofit showcase for the general public.

INFLUENCE PUBLIC POLICY

Could students use what they have learned to advocate for a change in policy?

Saving the Scrub Jay

Pelican Island Elementary School students in Florida made dozens of presentations to the school board, the Indian River County Commission, their U.S. Representative, and the Secretary of the U.S. Interior Department to demonstrate why the habitat of the scrub jay, an endangered species, needed protection. Ultimately, the Eco-Troop received a matching grant of more than $200,000 from the U.S. Fish & Wildlife Service to purchase undeveloped lots from private landowners for this wildlife sanctuary.

PHILANTHROPIC VENTURE

Could students write a grant or raise money to fund a project or social entrepreneurial venture?

Youth Philanthropy

Special education students at Langely Middle Schools developed a youth philanthropy program. A local foundation donated funds, but the students decided which organizations most deserved funding based on the needs they were addressing and their plan of action. Students learned how to create a grant proposal form, establish criteria to review the projects, and promote the opportunities in the community. They also learned how to monitor their budget and abide by legal issues. Students continue to raise funds by running a local coffee shop, and the profits keep resources flowing to needy nonprofits.

PROCESS- OR PROJECT-BASED SERVICE-LEARNING DESIGN

In addition to curriculum-driven service-learning design, teachers often use two general approaches to teaching service-learning. The first is process-based; start with a process (such as civic or scientific) and apply it to a problem. This approach allows students to connect an abstract process to a real problem they care about. Students see how helpful the process can be as it provides a helpful construct for examining a problem and taking action. If students use a scientific process, taking note of the steps and using the terms (*dependent variable, independent variable,* etc.), they are more likely to appreciate the process and understand its key elements. However, using a process to examine a problem that students care about and that involves the larger community often takes considerable time, and variables are less predictable, so the class may have to take more time engaging in the process. Teachers need strong facilitation skills to keep students on task and should explicitly draw connections to the scientific or civic process.

A good example of a process-based project is Project Citizen, in Touchet, Washington. Donnetta Elsasser's seventh grade class studied the effects of an overpopulation of mosquitoes and then took action. Floods had covered land in the area, resulting in so much standing water that the mosquitoes had multiplied and made it difficult for youth to play outside. After much discussion, the students developed an awareness campaign, met with the Mosquito Control District, and worked with county commissioners and other community groups. A public hearing is now scheduled for the summer, and the students will continue to be involved in carrying the issue to a vote. Working in cooperative teams, the class learned to interact with their government through a five-step process:

1. Identifying a public policy problem in their community;

2. Gathering and evaluating information on the problem;

3. Examining and evaluating solutions;

4. Selecting or developing a proposed public policy; and

5. Developing an action plan.

Another approach to service-learning is project-based—that is, choosing a project and letting the project's needs dictate the skills students learn. When multiple subjects are taught in the context of a project, students see how they naturally connect. Projects are built upon authentic learning activities that engage student interest and motivation. These activities are designed to answer a question or solve a problem and generally reflect the types of learning and work people do in the everyday world outside the classroom. These projects can often capitalize more on partnerships and more readily capture the imagination of students and community members. Students are more likely to master the skills because they will see an authentic context that requires them.

Research indicates that service-learning projects that last a semester are more impactful than shorter-term projects. Many educators, especially community-based youth leaders, prefer project-based service-learning. This approach allows students to focus on a project and learn or apply a variety of academic skills as they plan and implement the project. Instruction becomes more constructivist, and many teachers prefer being a facilitator of learning. The project-based method works best in schools that embrace content integration or project-based learning. However, this process frequently takes longer than estimated, and the variables of the project can be more difficult to control.

Hayes Bilingual Elementary School

In 2008, with the help of their teachers and the school librarian, students from both fifth grade classrooms participated in an ecological anthropology unit on the nearby Kinnickinnic River, a local waterway suffering from neglect and misuse as a dumping ground. Students focused on examining the relationship between Milwaukeeans and the urban river over the course of time. This project incorporated online learning and a multi-disciplinary approach, and was conducted in collaboration with such community partners as Friends of Milwaukee's Rivers, Sixteenth Street Community Health Center, The Park People of Milwaukee, and the University of Wisconsin–Milwaukee School of Architecture and Urban Planning. Students created a PowerPoint presentation to share with the wider community about the history of the river and to help raise awareness about what can be done to reduce pollution in the river. In addition to these advocacy efforts, students will be assisting with the layout for rain gardens at a local riverside park and creating information signage about the benefits of rain gardens. Their long-range goal is to have a bike path developed as a cooperative effort between community agencies and a local health clinic so the community can easily access a picnic area that will be established. The teacher developed a curriculum web that includes instruction in public speaking, math, civics, technology (PowerPoint), history, and literature.

WAYS TO STEP GENTLY INTO SERVICE-LEARNING

Consider your own comfort level with service-learning and be sure you are moving forward in a way that will be successful for you and your students. While many teachers are eager to leap in to take on a huge project, other teachers find it best to start small, perhaps with something they are already doing and simply explore ways a product or activity can be more directly connected to a community or school need.

Do your students already create a product or a performance?

An elementary art teacher already had her students making ceramic tiles. She met with her principal to explore how these tiles might be used at the school. She discovered that the public transit planned to decorate a bus stop across from their school and would be delighted to use her student's work. So her students interviewed community members and captured the history of their community in the tiles that now beautify the bus stop.

Can important skills or content be woven into an existing service activity?

A youth program had middle schoolers serve as mentors for elementary school members during the summer. The youth organization incorporated a well-designed tutoring program that reinforced the students' reading and writing skills, and they also focused on intentionally developing job readiness by having the middle school students apply and interview for the tutoring job and write a resume at the end of the summer. They also included a training session for the tutors as well as regular reflection and on-the-job training throughout the summer.

Can the work students are already doing be applied to a community need?

After a Head Start program learned that their middle school volunteers would be doing a research paper related to their service, the agency developed a list of research questions that would help their organization. A representative from Head Start provided a list of helpful resources, attended the student presentations, and made sure the information was passed on to the people who could do something with it.

Once started, these service-learning partnerships can become more robust over time as both the teacher and the partner become comfortable with their shared and distinct goals and more trusting of the process.

The possibilities for service-learning are endless, and students' passion and energy can often be the best guide.

NOTE TO YOUTH-SERVING ORGANIZATIONS

While this chapter focuses on core academic skills because schools are increasingly being held accountable for students' mastery of those skills, you can use the same processes to build more intentional connections between many of your program's learning goals—leadership, problem solving, cultural competency, interpersonal communication—and your service-learning projects. Students who are developing their leadership skills can teach these same skills to younger students as they learn about making healthy choices. They can develop creative ways to share this information with others or advocate for changes in policies.

Also, many community-based organizations are being asked to reinforce reading, math, writing, civic, health, and science competencies. These remediation or enrichment activities can have more impact if they are clearly aligned with the academic standards of the school, if students are able to learn more experientially through service-learning (cross-age teaching, project-based service-learning), and if students are able to teach these skills to others or apply the skills to new contexts. By combining positive youth development with intentional service-learning, youth development organizations are well positioned to help students make the personal and real connections to the content and concepts schools are teaching. For example, Camp Fire USA's new Hold On to Health curriculum reinforces health and civic skills as members advocate for easy access to healthy food for all people. If this reinforcement begins to use similar vocabulary and assessments to what schools use, it may help some students make more connections between learning in the classroom and learning in the community.

Whatever on-ramp you take to plan your project, you are responsible for meeting learning goals and expectations from a variety of different areas, including national and state standards, district expectations, community needs, and student interest. Organizing your plans at the outset can help you identify what academic expectations you hope to fulfill through this teaching method and begin thinking about the types of service that could help students meet the goal.

RESOURCES

GoToServiceLearning. This website highlights strong examples of service-learning that meet academic expectations and are designed to meet the Standards of High Quality Practice. At gotoservicelearning.org.

The National Service-Learning Clearinghouse. Check out the K–12 SLICE clearinghouse, where you can search by grade level and content area. At servicelearning.org.

Community Lessons: Integrating Service-Learning into the K–12 Curriculum, A Promising Practices Guide by Julie Bartsch profiles 14 service-learning projects with delineated connections to the Massachusetts State Frameworks. From the Massachusetts Department of Education at doe.mass.edu/csl/comlesson.pdf.

Boston Public Schools offers standards-based models created for teachers by teachers. Examples are divided into the following issue areas: citizenship, education, environment, human needs, and public safety with an emphasis on career development. At bostonteachnet.org/models2001.htm.

The KIDS Consortium, a service-learning nonprofit organization in Maine, features on its website model project ideas organized by subject matter. Each project description contains connections to Maine Learning Standards. At kidsconsortium.org.

The Service-Learning and Standards Toolkit features examples of actual service-learning curricula and assessments in use across the country. The toolkit also provides advice for using service-learning to help students achieve high academic standards. From the National Center for Learning and Citizenship of the Education Commission of the States. At ecs.org/clearinghouse/28/02/2802.htm.

The Complete Guide to Service-Learning: Proven, Practical Ways to Engage Students in Civic Responsibility, Academic Curriculum, and Social Action by Cathryn Berger Kaye, Free Spirit Publishing, illustrates ways to weave a variety of academic subjects into themes and civic issues that can serve as a focus for project-based learning.

The YMCA Service-Learning Guide: A Tool for Enriching the Member, the Participant, the YMCA, and the Community outlines three main components of the service-learning process: establishing learning objectives that are both broad and specific, performing meaningful service, and reflecting upon the experience so participants have a "snapshot" of what they have done. It provides real-life examples and ideas (mostly from YMCAs) that make the concepts of the three components easy to understand. Additionally, the guide includes assessment tools to explore project quality and sustainability, and other tips and resources related to service-learning.

The *Service-Learning and Standards Toolkit* features examples of actual service-learning curricula and assessments in use across the country. The Toolkit also provides advice for using service-learning to help students achieve high academic standards. From the National Center for Learning and Citizenship of the Education Commission of the States. At ecs.org/clearinghouse/28/02/2802.htm

Three Practical Resources for Linking Service-Learning and the Florida Sunshine State Standards details profiles of effective service-learning projects across subjects and grade levels, with a listing of standards that each project addressed. From Florida Learn and Serve. 240 pages. At fsu.edu/~flserve/sl/standards.html

Generating Service-Learning Ideas

What connections can you begin to make between your course or program learning goals and possible service-learning projects?

What particular portion of your curriculum has natural connections to the community? How can the skills students are learning be applied to issues that matter to them and the community?

What curricula theme or content area relates to an important community issue?

Are you finding that some academic standards are particularly difficult for students to learn, retain, or apply? Do you have an idea of certain standards on which students will not test well? How could these standards become relevant and applicable as students develop engaging ways to teach them to others or use them to complete "real work"?

Students retain more of what they teach to others. How could this be helpful in your program?

Is there some content that is boring to you or your students? How could it come alive as it is connected to real issues or helps create a more positive future for your school, your community, or the planet?

What compelling need does the school or community have?

Ask a community-based partner in a service-learning project how they can enrich students' learning while serving at their site.

What content or community issue are many of your students passionate about?

Learning Emphases in Different Settings

Examples of Possible Learning Emphases In ...

Service Project	YOUTH-SERVING ORGANIZATIONS	FAITH-BASED ORGANIZATIONS	SOCIAL SERVICE ORGANIZATIONS	SCHOOLS
Tutoring younger children	• Educational enrichment • Social skills (talking with younger children, problem solving, etc.)	• Developing qualities such as patience, listening, and caring	• The role of education in healthy development	• Mastery of specific reading strategies for both tutor and tutee • Vocabulary development
Studying and cleaning up a river or lake	• Appreciating nature • Responsibility for the environment	• A religious perspective on the environment	• Sustainable neighborhoods	• Scientific method for investigation and action • Application of math, scientific core content, and fiction and nonfiction reading skills
Participating in a voter registration drive	• Civic opportunity • Role organization • Commitment to the community	• The responsibility to participate in the political process	• Neighborhood organizing • Civic participation	• Voting registration process and regulations • Writing and reading literacy
Developing a presentation about racism	• Community organizing skills • Appreciating differences in society	• Religious perspectives of racial justice and reconciliation	• Community history with civil rights	• PowerPoint and oral presentation skills • Writing skills • Civic skills • Cultural competencies

(Adapted from Doing the Right Things Right: Using Quality Standards to Strengthen Community-Based Service-Learning) Search Institute. 2009 Learn and Service America's National Service-Learning Clearinghouse

Benefits and Challenges of Different Types of Service

Service activities can take many forms, from indirect service you perform within your organization to hands-on involvement and education and advocacy. Use ideas from this chart to identify possibilities that fit with your group's priorities, resources, and interests.

Benefits and Challenges of Different Types of Service

Type of Service:	EXAMPLES	BENEFITS	CHALLENGES
Indirect service: Activities that provide resources or services to others without any direct contact with the recipients	• Organizing a food drive • Collecting blankets and winter clothing for homeless people • Raising funds for organizations, causes, or disaster relief • Preparing food for a shelter • Creating care packages for new teen moms, refugees, or other groups in distress	• Meets important needs • Can build connections to distant places in the world • Does not require transportation	• Doesn't put young people directly in contact with recipients • Can perpetuate stereotypes or an "us and them" attitude about people being served
Direct service: Hands-on action on behalf of people or issues	• Assisting an elderly person or someone with a disability with shopping or other household tasks • Tutoring younger children • Helping immigrant families practice speaking and writing in English • Being a mentor to a younger child • Working on home repairs or construction of affordable housing	• Provides opportunities for relationship building • Can increase cross-cultural understanding • Personalizes social and justice issues by connecting them to individual people • Can offer immediate, tangible results	• Demands a stronger commitment from young people • Typically involves multiple visits over time or a extended experience • Usually requires transportation

continued →

Benefits and Challenges of Different Types of Service *cont'd*

Type of Service:	EXAMPLES	BENEFITS	CHALLENGES
Advocacy for social change: Speaking out on behalf of others and working to change the underlying conditions that keep them in need	• Sponsoring a voter registration campaign • Working to educate potential and current voters about issues • Writing letters to the editor or submitting articles about social issues to newspapers or other media • Participating in boycotts of goods or services that exploit vulnerable populations and/or harm the environment • Speaking up about social issues at town or committee meetings • Working on behalf of individual policy makers or other leaders	• Highlights justice issues for young people, reminding them of the systemic conditions that can perpetuate injustice • Gives young people experience in civic engagement and world issues	• Results almost never come quickly and may not be recognizable for years, if ever • Issues can be divisive and solutions complex • Some types of political involvement may be inappropriate for some groups
Education for change: Young people become catalysts for change by learning about social issues and sharing what they learn with others	• Develop a presentation about local hunger issues, HIV/AIDS education, or other themes • Compile and distribute a list of easily accessible resources for families in distress • Immersion opportunities where young people experience a different culture or setting in an intensive experience • Participating in community events and celebrations that honor the richness in the community's diversity	• Builds young people's information gathering and leadership skills • Positions young people as resources in their community • Provides the knowledge for young people to get more directly involved in issues and advocacy	• By itself, it does not provide direct contact with people in need • Can create conflict if issues are controversial

Roehlkepartain, E. C., Bright, T., Margolis-Rupp, B., & Nelson, L. I. (2000). *An Asset Builder's Guide to Service-Learning.* Minneapolis, MN: Search Institute.

Developing Service-Learning Partnerships

Just as it is important for students to value the service activity, it is important that the service-learning project is authentically valued by the larger community.

It's not uncommon for students to know little about their community needs or what makes their community a good place to live. Providing time for youth to learn more about their community's strengths and concerns can help them build relationships while working to identify what could be an important focus for their work.

CHOOSING A COMMUNITY ORGANIZATION

Most teachers start by finding an organization that can easily support their learning goals. While the possible partnerships are endless, it is important to develop a partner who genuinely values working with youth and who has a staff person who can champion the project. You also want a partner who would benefit from and value the research, direct service to clients, public awareness, advocacy, or products that youth can provide.

Some natural local partners can include:

- A neighborhood school or classroom
- Neighborhood associations, planning departments, city or community service programs, public health organizations, disaster preparedness programs, and chambers of commerce
- Arts organizations
- Volunteer centers or volunteer coordinator networks
- Veterans organizations

- Community action centers that coordinate many of the human services in a community

- Nonprofit organizations such as homeless shelters, Loaves & Fishes (loavesandfishes.org), the Humane Society (humanesociety.org), refugee support organizations, YWCA (ywca.org), Habitat for Humanity (habitat.org), and convalescent centers

- Local initiatives or coalitions that address issues such as affordable housing, afterschool programs, early childhood education, sustainability, local foods, health and wellness, public transit, and community arts

- City-sponsored youth commissions

- Library districts

- Museums

- County extension offices affiliated with land grant universities

- Local offices of federal departments (most federal agencies are encouraged to promote civic engagement)

- Local AmeriCorps programs (americorps.gov)

- College or university service-learning departments

- Faith-based organizations, including churches, synagogues, mosques, and local faith-based charities

- Youth-serving organizations such as YMCA (ymca.net), Camp Fire USA (campfireusa.org), Girl Scouts (girlscouts.org), Boys and Girls Clubs of America (bgca.org), and Big Brothers Big Sisters (bbbs.org)

- Service clubs, including Rotary (rotary.org), Kiwanis (kiwanis.org), Soroptimist (soroptimist.org), Lions Club (lionsclub.org), and Assistance League (assistanceleague.org)

- Private foundations

- Local businesses (businesses are frequently eager to partner with schools)

- National or global service-learning initiatives, such as
  - Earth Force (earthforce.org)
  - Humane Teen (humaneteen.org)
  - Youth Venture (youthventure.org)
  - In Our Global Village (inourvillage.org)
  - GenYes (genyes.com)
  - I*Earn (iearn.org)
  - Earth Echo (earthecho.org)
  - H2O for Life (h2oforlifeschools.org)
  - Special Olympics' Get Into It (getintoit.specialolympics.org)
  - Mercy Corps' Global Citizens (globalcitizencorps.org)

ESTABLISHING PARTNERSHIPS

A high-quality service-learning curriculum often benefits from a long-term partnership with community-based organizations and agencies. These partnerships help sustain the program by mobilizing shared knowledge, supervision, and resources. They also enable projects to be more likely to have more long-term impact on the community, and provide an authentic purpose and audience for student work. It is very important that the school and community partner are equally informed about the purposes and expectations of the projects.

The following recommendations for developing community partnerships were collected from experienced volunteer coordinators:

- Before your initial approach, do some research about the partner: know its mission, specific goals, and policies. Most organizations will have this information posted on a website.

- Community partners appreciate being included in the planning process. A face-to-face planning meeting makes all the difference, and helps with the development of trust.

- Be explicit and clear about your goals and expectations for the partnership. What will you provide to the organization? What do you hope they can provide to you?

- If you have specific elements that must be included in the project, mention those to the organization up front. Partners may need to adjust their expectations of the amount of work required, for example, if they learn that you will need time to have students do an on-site reflection piece, or journal entry.

- Look to your partner as a resource for your academic goals as well. Because they are so familiar with the elements of the *service* component, they may be able to provide you with suggested opportunities for making good academic connections.

- Be organized about your dates—and make sure to give your community partner plenty of advance notice. The more notice the partner gets, the better it will be able to accommodate working with you.

- Communicate roles clearly. Be explicit, both about the partnership and about the process. The partner will especially need to know about project leadership—will you want students to lead? Be clear, too, about follow-up to the meeting—who calls whom next?

- Not all prospective community partners have a full-time volunteer coordinator—and most organizations do not have staff dedicated to working with students. Do not assume that your community partner will understand how your school functions, know your school schedule, and so on. Especially note any "barriers," such as types of work that students should not be doing, limitations on time, and schedule conflicts.

- Community partners are used to working with adult volunteers, and will have "adult" expectations in mind when it comes to planning attendance and appropriate dress and behavior on site. Be prepared to reassure them that someone will be responsible for communicating these expectations to students and monitoring student behavior.

- Avoid endless "phone tag"—when you leave a message, state exactly when, where, and how (e-mail? phone?) it is easiest to reach you.

- Always respond to a contact from the community partner—especially if it involves the potential allocation of staff time or resources from the organization. If they don't hear from you, they will likely not go forward.

- Nonprofit organizations are usually well networked with one another; if one says that it cannot accommodate you, ask if it can recommend another organization with a similar mission.

- Always come through on your time commitment to the partner—this includes arriving on time, and staying through the time allotment you discussed in advance. The partner will plan a workload depending upon the number of anticipated volunteers and the amount of time available. Note that some partners may need to find replacements for late volunteers.

- Be sure to provide enough adults to supervise the student group. Ask the partner what the suggested adult/student ratio is, and be prepared to make suggestions based on your school or organization's protocols or requirements. Do *not* assume that the partner will provide staff (or volunteers) to fulfill that ratio. Do *not* show up with a group that is larger than the partner's maximum group size expecting that once your group is on site, the partner won't turn anyone away.

- Partners like hearing about the impact they have had. After the project is completed, encourage your students to share a reflective appreciation—a short note, or a link to a blog—with the partner.[1]

Burgerville Kids Meals

As part of a district-wide literacy project, an elementary school teacher and her students were interested in exploring ways their creative writing and visual art could reach the community. It was close to summer, and they thought it would be a good idea to encourage students to read during the summer. They partnered with Burgerville, a civically minded local restaurant that provides Kids Meals. The students convinced Burgerville to encourage summer reading. Students worked with an advertising/design company to design the bags for the Kids Meals and wrote a small book with activities that encouraged kids to read. For the month of July, literacy Kids Meals were sold at every Burgerville in Oregon and Washington.

IDENTIFYING COMMUNITY NEEDS

When service-learning is closely tied to content standards, the community partner may be defined by the learning goals. For example, if a class is studying the history of its community during World War II, the Veterans' Administration, local history museum, and neighborhood associations would be natural partners. If you are using a project-based approach, students need to investigate the community before determining the focus of their work and the roles of various partners. There are a variety of ways to identify the needs in a community, including surveys, collaboration with existing community programs, interviews with key people, examining data, and conducting a neighborhood assessment. Students often go to the community sites to interview community members or invite community representatives to have conversations with students at their school. The following methods not only help students identify a project that interests them but also enable the community to think more deeply about who they are and what they should be doing in order to have a greater impact on the community.

Possible Service-Learning Partners

What organizations are present in your community that might share
your learning and community goals?

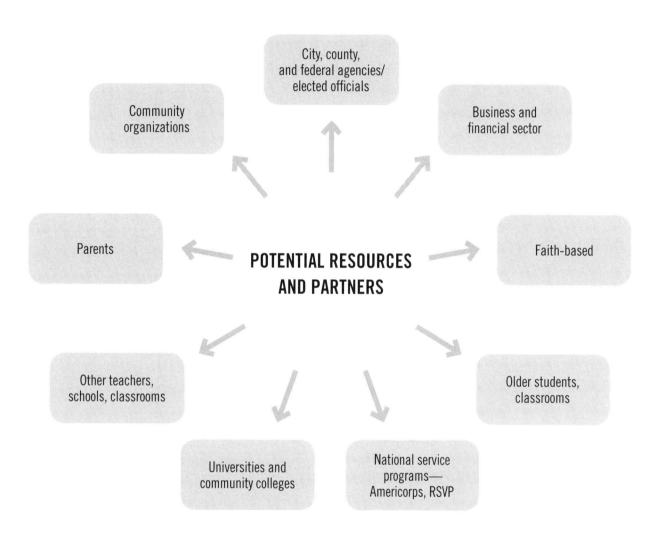

Questionnaire for Community Organizations

Name: _____ Contact Person: _____

Best way and time to contact: _____

What is the mission or purpose of the organization?

How does it serve the community?

Who funds and supports its work? How did it begin?

Is it a nonprofit, civic, for-profit, or faith-based organization?

What are your organization's current goals?

What challenges does your organization face in working toward its mission?

How does your organization currently involve young people?
What is effective about this current work?

What challenges have you faced in working with youth volunteers?

Are you familiar with the difference between volunteering and service-learning?

Do you have any service-learning partnerships with K–12 or college programs?

How might youth help your organization reach your current and future goals? How might youth help as volunteers, develop valuable products, expand your Web presence, conduct research, expand public awareness, create multilingual materials, help shape thoughtful public policy, or provide helpful input into planning?

What can the school and agency do to effectively prepare students so they can provide meaningful service?

What information do you have that will help me better understand your work and how to best partner with you?

What should our next steps be?

Examine Existing Data

Students can analyze data that has already been gathered by community groups by reviewing previous surveys and needs assessments. They can identify both authentic community needs and possible allies who can support their work.

Conduct Surveys

Students can design surveys for a variety of groups to gather information on what people see as important issues in their communities. Creating survey questions, deciding how to administer the survey, collating the resulting information, analyzing what the data show, and deciding how to act on that data can provide important real-world experiences for students. Audiences they might consider surveying include:

- Other students in the school
- Teachers and other school staff
- Community members or community organizations

Interview Community Members

The Inspired to Serve team developed some activities and a process that helps youth listen well as they interview community members. You will find these activities in "Exploring Your Community's Strengths and Hopes" by Eugene Roehlkepartain, a step-by-step guide for youth-led community listening projects. This guide provides youth with a way to see the strengths of their neighborhood and to engage in authentic conversations so they gain a deeper appreciation for people they only *think* they have always known.

Invite community elders and leaders into your classroom for interviews or discussions with students to explore topical areas or intergenerational or intercultural issues. Through preparing thoughtful questions, recording the information they learn, and analyzing what they've heard, students may find both areas of need they can address and partners to help them in their work.

Hold a Public Meeting

A public meeting allows participants to discuss local needs and explore possible actions. Some forums encourage a wide variety of community members to attend and express their ideas, while others, such as Seattle's annual Youth Summit, include only citizens 18 and younger.

Watershed Stewards

When a middle school science teacher decided to have his students observe and gather data on a stream that borders the school he realized he needed equipment and student supervisors. He contacted the county extension office to partner with Watershed Stewards, a program that provides equipment and training for students. Several Watershed Steward volunteers came on site with the students to provide supervision, and a retired teacher served as a mentor for both the middle school teacher and his students. Now every spring the students present their findings at the Watershed Congress that is sponsored by the City of Vancouver and the Clark County Water Resources Clean Water Program. Each year the program supports more than 1,000 students from 25 local Southwest Washington schools who monitor neighborhood streams, rivers, lakes, and wetlands. At the Watershed Congress, the focus is on education, discovery, and stewardship. Students ranging from third grade to twelfth grade present their water monitoring findings and engage in problem-solving sessions with other students and interested educators, community members, and professionals. Past Congress sessions have included presentations on a wide variety of watersheds.

TRANSFORMING COMMUNITY NEEDS INTO SERVICE-LEARNING PROJECTS

After students have identified genuine needs in their community, the next step is to consider how they can address that need through a service project, and how they can connect that service project to their overall learning goals. You can guide students in this process by making them aware of the learning goals they must achieve and then facilitating a brainstorming and decision-making process. The chart on the next page gives some examples of how needs can be transformed into projects with both a service and a learning component.

SELECTING A PROJECT

Perhaps the shape of the project has become very clear to you and your students as you've gone through a process of identifying needs and possibilities for meeting them, or maybe you have a number of possibilities—all of which may be viable. You can brainstorm a large list of those possibilities and options with the class, and then evaluate them for feasibility and interest. If you have a number of possible projects arising from your investigations, you can look at them through a variety of different frameworks to see if one jumps out as more viable than others.

Historical Preservation

Students from Pryor High School and Locust Grove Public Schools partnered with the Saline Preservation Association and other community partners to help save one of the only remaining nineteenth-century Cherokee district courthouses. Students helped educate and convince others of the importance of saving the Saline courthouse.

Guiding Questions for Teachers

- What project is most directly aligned with your content standards?
- What project would invigorate learning as it addresses an essential need?
- In what ways would you hope to make the community a better place by addressing this need?
- What will that look like? How will you know if you have been successful?
- What will you see, hear, and feel in the community?

Transforming Community Needs into Service-Learning Projects [2]

COURSE CONTEXT	COMMUNITY NEED	*How It Was Identified*	*Service Connected to Learning Goal*	*Learning*
Health—emergency health procedures	Local hospitals experience a shortage of blood.	Story in the local news	Students help run blood drives for the Red Cross, and create educational materials and presentations for peers, family, and community members on the importance of blood donation.	Biology of blood matching, persuasive writing and speaking, organizational skills
Social studies—how our community works	Bridging the age divide between older students and younger students in an elementary school	Classroom discussion on community	Sixth graders collect information about younger students through interviews and create "buddy books" to foster positive relationships between the grade levels.	Writing and conducting interviews, working on collaborative writing projects, improving interpersonal skills
U.S. history	Contemporary community lacks awareness of the stories of local veterans who served in conflicts.	Local historical society presented need and asked students for assistance.	Eighth graders visit with local members of the American Legion and gather information about serving the country in times of war. Students create documentaries about soldiers' lives that are archived at the historical society.	War and other armed conflicts in U.S. history, connecting individual stories of service to larger historical events, conducting interviews, creating narratives that combine historical information and personal stories
History of immigration in the US and language arts	Community is diversifying and lacks understanding of new cultural and ethnic groups.	News article on the increase of immigration and personal stories of conflict in the community	Seventh grade students study immigration in geography class, compare census statistics with a survey of their community, and involve community partners in creating a showcase of ethnic and cultural groups.	Students address geography and social studies standards, learning about the immigrant groups in their community and the cultural traditions.
Civics	Voter registration is low.	Statistics released from the Secretary of State's office and classroom discussion	After learning about voting trends and patterns in civics class, high school students design a voter registration drive. Students plan the campaign and partner with the League of Women Voters to increase awareness about upcoming elections.	Understanding elements of the election process, persuasive writing and speaking, cooperative learning and collaboration skills

- What possibilities are there for indirect service, direct service, advocacy for change, or educating others?

- What projects could young people initiate (such as organizing a campaign against texting while driving)? How might the project tie in to existing projects (for example, helping a local food shelf meet its mission)?

- What could individual students do on their own or in small groups? What kinds of projects would require a larger group of students or the whole classroom?

- What resources and constraints do you have to take into consideration? Help students think about how they fit in their community and the role your service-learning project might play. Taking time to explore these essential questions may better prepare students to define a plan of action.

RESOURCES

Building Community Through Service Learning: The Role of the Community Partner (2003). This ECS Issue Paper by Susan Abravanel highlights effective strategies for service-learning partnerships, using best-practice examples to illustrate potential impact. At ecs.org/clearinghouse/44/03/4403.pdf.

Exploring Your Community's Strengths and Hopes: A Step-By-Step Guide for Community Listening Projects. Community listening projects are beneficial in determining what a community's needs are prior to a service-learning project, and are a useful introduction to research processes for students. At servicelearning.org/filemanager/download/8842_communitylisteninginspiredtoserve.pdf.

Building Community: A Tool Kit for Youth and Adults in Charting Assets and Creating Change is a resource for youth and adult leaders, service-learning program coordinators, and anyone who is focused on generating and sustaining positive community development. At theinnovationcenter.org/files/BuildingCommunity_ToolKit.pdf.

Administrative Tip Sheets, Project Service Leadership: These tips distinguish different kinds of community partnerships that promote learning and clarify the step each partner needs to take in order to forge strong service-learning partnerships with higher education, business, and nonprofit organizations. At projectserviceleadership.org.

NOTES

1. Youth Service America, "Semester of Service Strategy Guide 2011," Washington, DC: Youth Service America, 2011: 41.
2. M. Wegner and C. Pernu, Eds., (Summer 2010) *The Generator* 28, no. 2., St. Paul, MN: National Youth Leadership Council.

Evaluating Project Possibilities

Use this form with some possible projects to narrow possibilities and make choices. If you don't know the answers to some questions, you may want to determine what they are before selecting a project.

Description of the Potential Project:

A. How well does the project address your goals for:
   1. Academic goals?
   2. Growth and development?
   3. Service?
   4. 21st century skills?
   5. Civic skills?
   6. Other academic standards?

B. How well does the project fit with your young people's:
   1. Interests and passions?
   2. Developmental stage and ability level?
   3. Life experiences and other differences?

C. How well does the project fit with the community's:
   1. Needs and priorities?
   2. Existing resources and programs?
   3. Experience and capacity in engaging young people in service?

D. How well does the project build upon your organization's:
   1. Mission or purpose?
   2. History and identity?
   3. Current projects and programs?
   4. Leaders' commitments and support?

E. Is the project appropriate for your group's:
   1. Size?
   2. Level of skill and experience?
   3. Time availability and commitment?

F. Will you be able to adequately address infrastructure issues such as:
   1. Funding?
   2. Risk management and safety?

G. Other:
   1.
   2.

Guiding Questions for Students

Use these questions to help you think about what kind of service-learning project you'd like to do.

Knowledge about Community

- What have you learned about your community so far?
- What new questions do you have about your community?
- What seems most important to do and why?

Personal Relationship

- What is your relationship to this community? How has it changed since you began thinking about how to serve it?
- Which projects would enable you to use the skills and knowledge you are using in this class?
- What could you do that would make you feel proud?

Partners

- Who in your community shares your ideals and values?
- Who might help you meet your obligations to the community?

Service

- How is the issue you will address personally relevant to you?
- How is it relevant to your community?
- Is it something that the people being served will recognize as important?
- Are the service activities you will do interesting and engaging?
- What will be the outcomes of the service? Will they be easily identified by others?
- What other questions or thoughts do you have about the service-learning project?

Youth Voice: Engaging Students and Lowering the Dropout Rate

Many teachers and even more youth-serving organizations have students take the lead in defining community needs and the specific academic content and skills that will be mastered or demonstrated by their service-learning projects. When students have more voice in the learning process, they are naturally more engaged and involved in what they are doing and learning. A recent telephone survey shows that students who had dropped out reported, among other reasons, that they lacked motivation and found that classes were boring. Another telephone survey shows evidence that service-learning can be a part of dropout prevention:

- Over 75 percent of students who were currently participating in or had in the past participated in service-learning programs agreed that service-learning classes were more interesting than other classes;

- Over 75 percent of service-learning students said service-learning has motivated them to work hard;

- Over 80 percent of students who participated in service-learning said they had more positive feelings about attending high school;

- About 45 percent of students who participated in service-learning believed that service-learning classes were more worthwhile than their other classes.[1]

MAKE IT MEANINGFUL TO STUDENTS

In order for service-learning to increase student engagement, students must value, for either intrinsic or extrinsic reasons, the service they are providing. While students may initially participate in an activity because they are getting additional points for their grades or because the teacher thinks it's a good idea, teaching and learning will not be transformed unless students discover that the skills and knowledge they are gaining are genuinely needed to address an authentic need.

You can make service-learning projects meaningful to students in a number of ways. Students can research possible community partners and identify two or three they'd like to work with, and then develop a list of questions for the potential community partner. Schedule at least one meeting between the students and community staff so students can ask questions. And before, during, and after the project, involve students in decision-making and leadership whenever practical.

The Pangaea Project

Every summer The Pangaea Project (thepangaeaproject.org) takes students from three high schools on an extraordinary learning expedition to Ecuador or Thailand. In preparation for their journey, participants meet daily for three weeks, developing trusting relationships with their adult team leaders and fellow students as they attend cultural sensitivity trainings, practice leadership skills, and learn about relief and development work. While abroad, students learn about the history, culture, and language of the country, explore the issues behind social and political situations, learn how to work as effective leaders with people unlike themselves by interacting cross-culturally, and develop leadership attributes including self-confidence, self-worth, and self-efficacy.

"Whereas prior to the involvement with The Pangaea Project, students frequently feel disempowered and disenfranchised and fail to see options for success, each Pangaea Project student exits our program knowing they have a future." —Stephanie Tolk, co-founder/resource development officer

WAYS SERVICE-LEARNING CAN LOWER DROPOUT RATES

Building Relationships

As teachers join students in completing projects that have value beyond the classroom, the classroom becomes socially engaging and students and teachers establish relationships in which they need each other to accomplish something worthy of their time. In diverse urban classrooms, where positive relationships between students and teachers and among students are particularly important, service-learning is a powerful tool to build the respectful relationships that are a prerequisite to instruction. As teachers become an ally to students who are engaged in real work, service-learning can transform the teacher's role from being the "evaluator" to coach.

Fostering a Sense of Personal Value

Community service and service-learning give young people access to two key resources: a feeling of usefulness and being valued, and a way to tangibly demonstrate to students that what they are learning is useful in the "real world."

Service-Learning Tools Series

Engaging Students in Reaching Out to Community Partners

The initial interaction between students and community partners will set the stage for the successful service-learning partnership. Students demonstrate the importance of youth voice in the following suggested process:

• Introduce students to local organization or agency partners

Present students with a list of – or have them research on their own – possible community partners. Ask students to identify two or three whom they would like to know more about, and possibly work with.

• What would you like to know ?

Have students develop a list of questions that they would have about the partner - what would they like to know about the organization/agency - and write it up as a survey to be presented to the partner. (see next page for sample questions)

• What service opportunities does this partner have for students ?

When the survey is presented (by students) to the partner, inform the partner that students would like to volunteer and provide service to the organization.

Give the organization specific guidelines about the possible project engagement:

how much time they would have from the students

your goals in having a learning connection for the activity

the need to involve a reflective piece (and therefore to allow for time for this)

celebrating student success following the activity

Invite the partner to prepare two or three possible options to propose to students for their engagement (giving students another opportunity for student voice, as they "choose" the project).

• Planning for a school visit

Invite the partner to come to school to meet with the students, to be prepared to answer student questions about the organization, and to present and discuss the options for a service activity.

Once students have selected the project activity, invite them to brainstorm with the organization representative what they will need to do in order to coordinate with the organization to accomplish the project. Depending on your level of confidence in the students, you may choose to have them assume responsibility for pieces of developing the relationship with the partner.

© SOLV 2008 ◆ (503) 844-9571 / (800) 333-SOLV ◆ www.solv.org

Helping Students Learn About Agencies/Organizations

The following are suggested "starter" questions that students might have about agencies or organizations, as they begin the process of developing a partnership for service-learning.

- What is the purpose of the agency/organization?

- How does it contribute to the life of our community?

- What is the history of the organization – how, when and why did it get started?

- What kind of organization is it?
  Non-profit (independent sector)? For profit (private sSector)? Civic (public sector)?

- Who makes the important decisions for the agency/organization ?

- What public policies shape or influence its work?

- What is its vision for the future?

- How is it funded?

- What programs does it offer?

- Why did it choose to focus on those programs?

- How do volunteers participate in this organization?

- Are young people involved with the organization ?

- Is it possible for students to have a role in planning or implementing programs with this organization ? How would this work ?

- How do you think young people could play a larger role in helping this organization?

© SOLV 2008 ◆ (503) 844-9571 / (800) 333-SOLV ◆ www.solv.org

Understanding the Continuum of Youth Involvement

	PARTICIPATION ➡	VOICE ➡	LEADERSHIP ➡	ENGAGEMENT
YOUTH ROLES	Youth are involved in the "doing" of the activity but not in the planning, development or reflection.	Youth are part of conversations regarding planning and implementing an idea. Their input is considered, but they may or may not have an official "vote".	Youth are involved at all levels of idea or project development and have formal and informal leadership roles in the process.	Youth are the primary drivers of the work from conceptualization to implementation and reflection. Youth "own" and understand the work deeply.
ADULT ROLES	Adults develop the idea, plan and organize all aspects of the activity or event which a cadre of young people will actually carry out.	Adults develop and set the agenda and facilitate the process. Adults include the input of youth in this process. This can be through consideration of youth input via focus group or meeting or through youth being involved in and having a formal vote.	Adults are involved in the full process and support the development of individual youth and the flow of the process, but in a way that balances power and leadership with youth. Adults allow youth to struggle and make mistakes in a safe environment.	Adults provide a support role and share ownership and commitment but with some deference to the youth. Adults hold one "vote" on the team.
DECISION-MAKING	Adults make all decisions.	Adults ultimately make the decision with the consideration of youth input. If youth have a vote, they are typically outnumbered or adults have ultimate veto power.	Youth and adults share decision-making power often requiring a specific and mutually agreed upon decision-making process.	Youth ultimately make the decisions with the inclusion of adult input and "vote".
ACCOUNTABILITY	Adults are accountable for all aspects of the process and/or activity including whether or not young people are present. Youth have some secondary accountability to participate in the activity.	Adults maintain accountability for decision-making and actions. Youth may have specific accountability for smaller roles and activities that involve youth specifically.	Youth and adults share accountability at all levels of the work.	Youth have primary accountability at all levels of the work. Adults have secondary accountability for ensuring that youth are prepared and supported in a way that they can achieve success.
EXAMPLE	School leadership is holding a student assembly to raise awareness about how the school engages students with disabilities. A group of students is asked to pass out flyers and to serve as hosts and to introduce the special speaker for the assembly.	School leadership wants to improve how they engage students with disabilities in the classroom and broader school activities. They have invited two youth to ***participate*** on a task force of faculty and staff to develop a list of ideas for action.	Students want to raise awareness about challenges for students with disabilities in their school. They get an adult sponsor who gets the OK for them to have school assembly on the issue and have an expert speaker come. Youth ***participate and have voice*** in the planning and development of the assembly by serving on committees, as a committee chair, introducing the speaker, promoting the event etc.	Youth plan, organize all aspects of, and host a student assembly focused on more equitable schools for students with disabilities. They ask a supportive teacher to serve as an advisor. They know the issue deeply and have talked with their peers including students with disabilities to garner insight. They have developed ideas for school improvement that they message to their peers and to school leadership directly.

Contact: Anderson Williams
awilliams@oasiscenter.org

Follman and Muldoon (1997) reported that "Because a sense of empowerment and playing useful roles in society may be in shorter supply for low-SES students, service and service-learning may have a greater influence among socioeconomically disadvantaged students on the constellation of factors that affect academic success. . . . Students' school attendance increased on days when they had service-learning, with the interpretation that on those days the students realized that to skip school would be to disappoint the service recipients with whom they feel connected."[2]

Math Games

Teacher Mary Stell transformed the culture of her special education and low-achieving math classroom. Rather than filling her class time with lots of rote tasks, her students developed learning games and activities to teach basic math procedures to elementary students. It was challenging for them to develop fun, engaging, and effective games that would help "their students" master and apply key concepts. When they learned that their fourth and fifth graders outscored other students they were thrilled because it indicated that their math games and tutoring had been genuinely helpful, and their own test scores improved over non-service-learning students. These students, who are at high risk of dropping out, are now " the teachers" at the neighboring elementary school. The partner school so valued the services the students are providing that they reorganized their schedules so all their fifth graders could benefit from assistance next year.

Curricular Connections

As service-learning connects academic content to real-world needs, the context for learning changes. This is particularly valuable to those students who are the least engaged with traditional curriculum. The purpose of service-learning is no longer simply for a grade; instead it is to do something that matters to people who matter to them or that can change things that are of concern to them.

In his research of effective high school instruction, Fred Newman discovered that students are more engaged when learning tasks require complex thinking and when there is an audience beyond the classroom for the work they are doing. Research indicates that service-learning can embody these important components because it

- Highlights ways learning can be applied in real-life situations;
- Helps students feel that their schoolwork is significant, valuable, and worthy of their efforts;
- Gives students some degree of control over their own learning;
- Assigns challenging but achievable tasks;
- Stimulates students' curiosity about the topic being studied; and
- Designs projects that allow students to share new knowledge with others.[3]

Empowerment

Service-learning projects can teach youth to solve not only immediate needs, but look at the issues underlying those needs, which leads to a greater sense of empowerment. For example, youth working with a local food bank learn that they can help feed families and individuals, but also have the opportunity to explore issues of power and the socio-political factors that contribute to issues of hunger and homelessness. Exploring how other communities or countries approach this same dilemma and how they can work to make more systemic changes empowers students with an increased civic knowledge and sense of efficacy.

Matanzas Legacy Project

While the intensity and duration of a service-learning project are always important, when a project involves students who are likely to drop out, they are essential. Only by putting in time together can the relationships and skills be built for young people to have the competence and confidence they need to take the risk of action.

The Matanzas Legacy Project in Flagler County, Florida, is a service-learning partnership that mutually benefits students, the community, the school district, and the environment. The Princess Place Preserve is a tract of over 1,500 acres composed of diverse ecosystems that include saltwater marshes, freshwater wetlands, mature oak hammocks and pine communities, scrub habitats, and an adjacent estuary. Every day, students in a dropout prevention program travel by bus to Princess Place. Students monitor water quality, inventory plants, publish interpretive materials, develop trails, design and post interpretive signage for trails and butterfly gardens, and give tours and lessons to other students and the larger community. During its first nine years, every student in the program graduated—an unprecedented achievement with such a highly at-risk population.

Further program examples can be found at projectserviceleadership.org in the Learn, Serve, Succeed section.

RESOURCES

Raising Their Voices: Engaging Students, Teachers, and Parents to Help End the High School Dropout Epidemic by John Bridgeland, Robert Balfanz, Laura A. Moore, and Rebecca S. Friant. Report by Civic Enterprises in Association with Peter D. Hart Research Associates. March 2010.

Engaged for Success: Service-Learning as a Tool for High School Dropout Prevention by John M. Bridgeland, John J. DiIulio Jr., and Stuart C. Wulsin. Report by Civic Enterprises in association with Peter D. Hart Research Associates for the National Conference on Citizenship. April 2008.

National Dropout Prevention Center is a resource center for dropout prevention strategies and practical service-learning resources. At dropoutprevention.org.

America's Promise. Grad Nation is a national movement to mobilize Americans to end the high school dropout crisis and prepare young people for college and the 21st-century workforce. It's a call to action for concerned citizens, businesses, community leaders, policy makers, educators, and the nation. At americaspromise.org/Our-Work/Grad-Nation.aspx.

National Youth Leadership Council sponsors The Generator School Network and the Urban Institute to help teachers working with students who are at risk for dropping out. They also offer a toolkit that focuses on dropout prevention. At nylc.org.

NOTES

1. J. Bridgeland, J. DiIulio, and K. Morison, *The silent epidemic: Perspectives of high school drop-outs,* Washington, DC: Civic Enterprises, 2006.
2. P. C. Scales, E. C. Roehlkepartain, M. Neal, J. Kielsmeir, P. Benson, "Reducing Academic Achievement Gaps: The Role of Community Service and Service-Learning," *Journal of Experiential Education* 29, no. 1 (2005).
3. S. J. Meyer, L. Hofshire, and S. H. Billig, "The impact of service-learning on MEAP: A large scale study of Michigan Learn and Serve grantees, year two evaluation report," Denver, CO: RMC Research Corporation, 2004.

Diversity and Cultural Competence

In communities that have a strong sense of cultural identity, service-learning has the potential to affirm the value of this culture. Service-learning can open the classroom to the community and the community to the classroom. This increases the positive interactions between supportive adults and children and potentially reduces the sense of separation between schools and students' lives.

And when service-learning is tightly connected to the cultural community with which the adolescent identifies, it is more likely to foster Developmental Assets. If the classroom teacher is not part of the cultural community that is central to the student's life, it is even more important that the service-learning activities are tightly woven with the cultural community. When done well, culturally rich service-learning will be uniquely supported by the family and community, the positive values of their community will be affirmed, and youth are more likely to develop a positive identity as they work with the adults and community leaders with whom they identify.

Effective service-learning shares some of the key elements of Culturally Responsive Teaching.[1]

In a recent study of classroom practice in diverse urban schools, Jeff Duncan-Andrade found that several practices were common among effective teachers. These same ideologies and pedagogies can help service-learning practitioners determine if they can effectively use service-learning in a cultural context. Dr. Duncan-Andrade found that teachers who were effective in urban schools

- Believe their students, specifically low-income children of color, comprise the group most likely to change the world. To prepare fertile ground for *all* their students to succeed, particularly the students who would be risk takers, these teachers worked at understanding the history of the communities where they worked and the people who live there.

Elements Shared by Service-Learning and Culturally Responsive Teaching

ELEMENTS OF CULTURALLY RESPONSIVE TEACHING	ELEMENTS OF EFFECTIVE SERVICE-LEARNING
Establish the purpose of what is being learned and its relationship to the students' cultural experiences.	Using classroom skills to enhance service to the community gives students a greater purpose for learning.
Share the ownership of learning and knowledge among all students.	As students, community members, and teachers work together to develop meaningful community service connections to classroom learning, students feel more ownership of their education.
Assume a hopeful and respectful view of people.	As students engage in projects that improve the community they see concrete ways they can contribute to their community and often choose to take on greater leadership roles.
Treat all students equitably.	As teachers and community members see that students have talents and skills that can help the community, students become increasingly viewed as resources.
Develop positive relationships. Relate teaching and learning activities to students' experiences or previous knowledge in content and assessment methods based on their experiences, values, needs, and strengths.	Service-learning experiences require students to use their classroom skills in a community setting and students are often encouraged to choose and design projects that have personal value.
Enhance meaning. Provide challenging learning experiences involving higher-order thinking and critical inquiry.	Students engage in environmental, intergenerational, and cultural projects that stimulate critical inquiry and reflective thinking skills.
Engender competence. Connect the assessment process to the students' world and frames of references.	Involving ethnic communities in designing, implementing, evaluating values, and celebrating the work of young people helps connect students' actions to the communities with which they identify.
Encourage self-assessment.	A central part of the service-learning process is reflection, which encourages students to examine what they are learning about the community and themselves as they complete their project.

■ Talk to students about using school as a way to return to their communities rather than a strategy for escaping them.

■ Believe that education is "a part of a path to freedom." If students can learn the skills teachers are trying to build for them, they will be in a better position to think and act critically for themselves and for their community.

■ Are committed to being a consistent presence in the school community and the lives of the students and their families. They described their decision to become members of the communities where they taught as part of a commitment to solidarity with their students, as opposed to empathy for them.

- Have a distinct commitment to building trust with their students. These teachers understand that government institutions, such as schools, have a negative history in poor and nonwhite schools. No matter how good their intentions, they are aware that as ambassadors of the institution of school they are connected to that history. This awareness allows them to be conscious of this obstacle to building trust with students and the community and also helps them understand the importance of standing in opposition to school policies that are oppressive, racist, and colonist, and that perpetuate the cycles of inequality.[2]

Cherokee Nation Learn and Serve

Addressing a need to enhance social awareness and reduce risky behavior among youth, the Cherokee Nation Learn and Serve connected young people to work with community elders to restore the value of Cherokee life-ways and the practice of "Ga du gi" (working together for the good of all). More than 3,000 students and 500 adults participated in service activities organized by Cherokee Heritage Service Clubs. A Tribal Youth Council will act as ambassadors to expand service-learning into new school sites, and an Elders' Council advised teachers and students on cultural values such as sharing, respect, cooperation, and inclusion.

STANDARDS OF PRACTICE: DIVERSITY

To implement high-quality service-learning in diverse cultural communities, teachers need to pay special attention to the Diversity and Community Partnerships standards mentioned in Chapter 1. The following pages outline some strategies that can guide effective implementation of these standards.

- Explore with leaders of a local ethnic community the traditions of service that have been part of their ethnic heritage. Ask how leaders experienced service during their youth and discuss how service-learning revisits traditional ways of becoming an adult.

- Encourage students to become involved in service opportunities that are valued by their families or communities (for example, students might provide service to an elder or help at tribal activities).

- If the program includes youth from various cultures, carefully prepare students to work together with people of different backgrounds. Discuss the fact that cultural backgrounds and ethnic identity are important determinants of attitudes, values, and behaviors in social settings and prepare community partners to successfully interact with one another.

- Introduce service at an early age. Service-learning programs involving children in preschool and kindergarten can be specifically designed to reduce prejudice.

- Encourage projects that eventually call students to work in diverse teams toward a concrete, shared goal. Be sure all students have been prepared so they have the competence they need for the project to be successful. All students should start the project on equal footing with their peers.

Service-Learning Tip Sheet
Diversity

Effective service-learning values diversity in its participants, practice, and outcomes. Understanding diversity and its impact on service-learning is critical for effective practice.

Diversity refers to the variety of abilities, and social and cultural heritages within a group or community. Service-learning promotes diversity by:

Reflecting Common Cultural Values
Every culture uniquely values service to others. Service-learning offers an opportunity for every student to express core cultural values.

Emphasizing Each Student's Capacities
All learners can make a contribution through service programs; all talents, skills, and experiences are valuable and necessary.

Building Capacity for Action
Working toward a common goal through service-learning enables those with varying abilities, races, religions, and cultural orientations to share a common experience that serves as a basis for developing friendships. It cultivates a capacity for cooperating, making a difference, and meeting real needs.

Enlarging Perspectives
Learning different ways to accomplish tasks and solve problems during reflection sessions builds positive relationships with peers and adults, and develops a sense of shared citizenship.

Reinforcing Positive Identity
Valuing differences reinforces self-worth and self-esteem.

Promoting Humane Values
Becoming aware of problems encountered by those who have different abilities and cultural backgrounds helps develop sensitivity to these issues. Direct interaction with the community helps dispel misconceptions.

Engaging Learners and Encouraging Educational Excellence
Interacting with others in new and unfamiliar environments reinforces the relevance of academic subjects taught in school, and allows students to build on past experiences with new learning.

Performing Valuable Service
Becoming aware of community needs leads to developing effective ways to respond to them.

Available from the NYLC Resource Center at www.nylc.org.
Adapted from "Getting Started in Service-Learning."
Copyright © 2005 National Youth Leadership Council. All Rights Reserved.

www.nylc.org

National Youth Leadership Council
1667 Snelling Avenue North
Suite D300
Saint Paul, MN 55108

NYLC Tip Sheets are funded by the State Farm Companies Foundation.

Cultural Community Partners

When members of students' cultural community play a central role in planning, executing, and celebrating a service-learning project, students experience a greater sense of accomplishment and view school as integral to their lives. Forging partnerships with cultural organizations takes time because participants must establish a sense of mutual respect during the current efforts and, at the same time, acknowledge and "release" past efforts or failure

Cultural partners can specifically help draw real-world application and practicality to the curriculum and emphasize the importance of the cultural piece for student success and engagement. They can help develop curriculum that honors various cultures in the classroom, and sensitize teachers to cultural implications for parents and students.

The following strategies can guide you through effective implementation of the diversity standard.

- Take time to develop relationships with ethnic leaders who are part of your school's community. (For example, visit community agencies or tribal gatherings to gain a better understanding of the cultural history and significance of local ethnic leaders.)
- Explore ways to engage families. View all people as resources.
- Seek higher-education partners. They can play additional roles depending on the need of the school and its students. Higher-education partners provide assistance in three key ways. They (1) develop and assist in implementation with measurements and assessments, (2) provide sustainability and consistency among community partners, and (3) provide resources in understanding the culture and connecting with the community.[3]

GETTING STARTED

Think about which groups in your community have full membership and which are marginalized, and encourage community connections and service projects that are inclusive. Also examine your expectations regarding learning from, as well as about, traditionally marginalized groups. Efforts to establish relationships with historically marginalized communities can often be seen as paternalistic rather than respectful, so ensure that you actively create a power-sharing relationship. Think about issues that are valuable to both sides that you can explore together.

AASK (Aardvarks Advocate Skills and Knowledge)

High school students from Oregon Episcopal School and AASK graduates explore the social justice issues behind literacy and equity as they work with Spanish-speaking students from grades 3 through 8 at Vose Elementary and Whitford Middle School. One of the unique characteristics of the program is that everyone, whether volunteer high school staff or the elementary and middle school AASK students, are equal partners in the program: everyone is learning and serving side-by-side. The high school volunteers learn patience, empathy, and Spanish as they tutor, and the elementary and middle school students gain stronger reading, writing, and math skills in English. Learning about each other's families, schools, and customs encourages deeper understanding that gives way to strong personal relationships that honor differences in age, race, and culture. Because the program leaders regularly reflect on their own practice and participate in cultural competency professional development, the program design and training is continually improving.

Further resource and program examples can be found at projectserviceleadership.org in the Learn, Serve, Succeed section.

RESOURCES

How Service-Learning Complements Multicultural Education by Stella Raudenbush, MacClellan Hall, David Koyama, and Kate McPherson. Project Service Leadership, 1998.

The Intercultural Communication Institute sponsors the Summer Intercultural Institute of Communication, which focuses on a variety of topics, from intercultural communication styles to racial identity in America. They also have an Intercultural Foundations certification program, and a Masters in Intercultural Relations. At nonprofitoregon.org/about.

National Indian Youth Leadership Project, Inc., has a mission to nurture the potential of Native youth to be contributors to a more positive world through adventure-based learning and service to family, community, and nature. At niylp.org.

Interfaith Youth Corps builds mutual respect and pluralism among young people from different religious traditions by empowering them to work together to serve others. At ifyc.org.

K–12 Get Into It, part of the Special Olympics program, offers service-learning activities that can be completed in a classroom or community setting, as part of a club, as an afterschool activity, or as a community-based event. Activities include involvement with local Special Olympics programs whenever possible. At getintoit.specialolympics.org.

Culturally Responsive Standards-Based Teaching: Classroom to Community and Back by Steffan Saifer, Keisha Edwards, Debbie Ellis, Lena Ko, and Amy Stuczynski. Corwin Publishing, 2010.

"Service-learning and multicultural/multiethnic perspectives," by W. Weah, V. C. Simmons, and M. Hall. *Phi Delta Kappan,* May 2000: 673–675.

NOTES

1. R. J. Wodkowski and M. N. Ginsberg, "A Framework for Responsive Teaching," *Educational Leadership* 53, no. 1 (September 1995).
2. J. Duncan-Andrade, "Gangstas, Wankstas and Ridas: Defining, developing and supporting effective teachers in urban schools," *International Journal of Qualitative Studies in Education* 20, no. 6 (November 2007): 617–638.
3. T. Lennon, *Service-Learning and Hispanic Students: What Works in the Field,* Denver, CO: Education Commission for the States, 2009.

Civic Education

Schools and community organizations are finding that service-learning is a key ingredient for effective civic education and is essential for districts to fulfill their civic mission. This chapter will feature service-learning that has been effectively combined with citizenship instruction to prepare young people in the following three areas:

1. **Civic literacy**—Fundamental knowledge of history and government, political and community organizations, and public affairs; skills for making informed judgments; engaging in democratic deliberation and decision-making; influencing the political process; and organizing within a community.

2. **Civic virtues**—Values, beliefs, and attitudes needed for constructive engagement in the political system and community affairs, such as tolerance, social trust, and a sense of responsibility for others.

3. **Civically engaged behaviors**—Habits of participating and contributing to civic and public life through voting, staying politically informed, and engaging in community service.

Well-designed service-learning activities that effectively foster civic skills have been shown to increase several student capabilities, including their knowledge of community needs, their awareness of social problems and acceptance of diversity, and their sense of personal and social responsibility. In addition, civic service-learning enhances students' knowledge of government, fosters their willingness to work toward social change, and increases their involvement in and commitment to service.

The service-learning programs that are most effective for civic education are known to

■ Encourage teachers and administrators to consciously pursue civic outcomes and not merely seek improved academic performance or higher self-esteem.

- Allow students to engage in meaningful work on serious public issues, with a chance of seeing positive results within a reasonable amount of time.

- Give students a role in choosing and designing their projects and strategies.

- Provide students with opportunities to reflect on the service work and draw specific connections to the roles and responsibilities of citizenship.

- Link service with specific civic skills and knowledge.

- Allow students—especially older students—to pursue political responses to problems (e.g., contacting local officials), consistent with laws that require public schools to be nonpartisan.

- Deliberately focus on civic outcomes such as students' propensity to vote, work on local problems, join voluntary associations, and follow the news.

- Advocate that their students personally participate in politics and civil society, including at the local level, although without advocating a particular position or party.

- Engage students in discussions of issues and participate in activities that can help put a "real life" perspective on what is learned in class. These activities can range from collaborative research projects and presentations to simulations, mock elections, service-learning projects, and participation in student government.

- Emphasize ideas and principles that are essential to constitutional democracy.

In 2002 the Carnegie Corporation gathered scholars, researchers, educators, and government leaders to discuss and examine the current state of civic education in our country. A report by this group, the Civic Mission of Schools (CMS), currently guides local state and national policy on civics in our schools.

The Civic Mission of Schools recommended that schools:

— 1 —

Provide instruction in government, history, law, and democracy.

Project Citizen

Although Project Citizen, developed by the Center for Civic Education, can be used in many settings, it's most often incorporated into secondary social studies, civics, or government classes. The project follows a three-step process:

1. Facilitate a discussion about a school or community problem that can be improved through a change in policy;

2. Study the issue and decide on a plan of action; and

3. Implement the plan.

Classrooms across the country are investing and influencing state and federal policies. For example, Patty McMaster's class at Evergreen High School (Vancouver, WA) wrote a bill to require the teaching of state government and politics in Washington State schools. Her students helped support the passage of House Bill 2781, which ensures that Washington State History—a required class—includes instruction on the state's economy, constitution, and geography. The bill was unanimously passed and went into effect on the class graduation day.

City Works (a program of the Constitutional Rights Foundation)

City Works infuses the study of local government into mainstream government or civics courses. A civic-engagement component involves students in projects that address community issues. Students also document and evaluate their experiences. When students complete this unique curriculum, they have developed a deeper understanding of local government and the role they can play as citizens.

— 2 —
Incorporate discussion of current issues and events in the classroom, particularly those that young people view as important to their lives.

Earth Force at Holland Middle School

Students at this middle school decided they wanted to address an environmental issue at their school. They began by conducting a survey of students and educators. Once they analyzed the results they found that a key concern at their school was energy use. The students worked with their social studies teacher to understand policy-making at their school. Once they had identified a problem they were going to address, they used a number of different tools to get their message out, including PowerPoint presentations, flyers, commercials, and announcements that were distributed all over the school to remind students and staff to conserve energy. Some students even taught classes on energy conservation to elementary students.

— 3 —
Design and implement programs that provide students with the opportunity to do community service that is linked to the formal curriculum and classroom instruction.

ACT/Active Citizenship Today

For more than a decade, the Active Citizenship Today (ACT) program has offered an exciting approach to civic education through service-learning. The newly revised ACT curriculum helps students develop citizenship skills and knowledge while they plan and implement service-learning projects.

Freedom Schools' Junior Leader Program

Participation in Philadelphia's Freedom Schools' Junior Leader Program, in which students participated in a year-long service-learning project on community issues, increased in measures of connection to the community, connection to American society, making community changes, and developing leadership skills.

—— 4 ——
Offer extracurricular activities that provide opportunities for young people to get involved in their schools or communities.

Youth in Government

YMCAs across the country offer a Youth in Government Program that provides students the opportunity to experience the democratic process firsthand. Throughout the year, participants learn how to research public policy issues, write real legislation, practice public speaking and debating skills, and work together to achieve a goal. Assuming the roles of senator, representative, lobbyist, and press, the Youth Legislature meets in a four-day legislative session presided over by their statewide elected officials, including governor, Secretary of State, lieutenant governor, and Speaker of the House.

UNITY (United Nation Indian Tribal Youth)

In an unprecedented move of solidarity, Native youth representing several tribal nations are calling upon the White House to help them address the alcohol, drug, and other substance abuse issues they face. More than 1,200 youth representing youth councils across 35 states unanimously passed a resolution at the 2010 National UNITY Conference in San Diego, California.

Illinois Youth Summit

The Illinois Youth Summit combines discussion with service. Each year, the Summit focuses on issues chosen by students from a list provided by policy-makers and educators. This year students selected issues related to the balance of freedom and safety after 9/11. In preparation, they spent weeks in law and government classes conducting surveys, reading, and practicing discussion skills. At the Summit, students came together to discuss the chosen issues with key policy-makers and students from other schools. Participating classes also taught other classes, wrote to newspapers and policy-makers, or prepared instructional materials for cable TV.

—— 5 ——
Encourage student participation in school governance.

Secondary Academy for Success

Students at the Secondary Academy for Success (SAS), a public alternative high school in the Bothell School District, participated in a series on SoundOut Student Voice Forums. They recorded interviews they had with teachers regarding how the school could be improved and then presented their findings to the school's School Improvement Planning committee. Their thoughts were incorporated into the school's plan, and students continued to be involved in school building design plans. Today the legacy of the forums continues, and student voice has a strong role at SAS.

School-Wide Community Councils: Hudson High School

In September 2003, Hudson High School in Hudson, MA, launched two new civic development efforts—clustering and school-wide governance—that provide an opportunity to study the influence of school-wide democratic deliberation on students' civic knowledge and participation. The intervention involved, in part, organizing the school into clusters of 100 to 150 students that meet for one hour each week to discuss governance and other school-related issues, perform community service, and pursue other cluster-related activities. Successive classes of twelfth graders showed improvements on measures of community service and political knowledge, and the improvements were widespread in the student population.

RESOURCES

CIRCLE (The Center for Information and Research on Civic Learning and Engagement) promotes research on the civic and political engagement of young Americans. CIRCLE conducts and funds research with practical implications for those who work to increase young people's engagement in politics and civic life. CIRCLE is also a clearinghouse for relevant information and scholarship. At civicyouth.org.

Center for Civic Education promotes responsible participation in civic life by citizens committed to values and principles fundamental to American constitutional democracy, including civic education, law-related education, and international educational exchange programs for developing democracies. CCE is the source of two widely used civics curricula, "Project Citizen" and "We, The People," as well as the document, "Civitas: A Framework for Civic Education." CCE's website includes numerous ideas for lesson plans and activities to promote civic skills. At civiced.org.

Character Education Partnership (CEP) is a nonpartisan coalition of organizations and individuals dedicated to developing moral character and civic virtue in our nation's youth as one means of creating a more compassionate and responsible society. At character.org.

The National Assessment of Educational Progress (NAEP) Civics Report Card presents the results of the 2006 national assessment of what U.S. students in grades 4, 8, and 12 know and can do in civics. At nationsreportcard.gov/civics_2006.

National Center for Learning and Citizenship (NCLC) is a project of the Education Commission of the States (ECS) and has developed several useful publications about civic education for state education policy makers, many of which highlight the educational value of service-learning. Publications include "Citizenship Matters," a monthly newsletter, and "Every Student a Citizen: Creating the Democratic Self." At ecs.org/nclc.

Facing the Future works within the education system to help teachers help students achieve academic success, while preparing them to create and maintain positive, healthy, and sustainable communities. At facingthefuture.org.

Civic Responsibility Meter

Developed by John Minkler and Don Hill

When service-learning supports some of the thirteen civic education components listed below, it is a teaching strategy that helps youth learn to become contributing citizens in a democratic society. One way to identify the degree of civic responsibility in a service-learning project is to consider its contribution to these components.

Instructions: Rate each of the 13 components of civic responsibility in a project or program with 0 to 3 check marks.

_____ = Not Present   _✓_ = Present   _✓✓_ = Strong   _✓✓✓_ = Very Strong

Civic Knowledge

1. _____ Builds knowledge of school, local, state, or federal government structures and functions.

2. _____ Builds knowledge of democratic principles and U.S. founding ideals.

3. _____ Develops understanding and knowledge of exemplary role models (historic or current).

Problem-Solving Skills

4. _____ Develops skills of critical thinking, research, and analysis of current issues.

5. _____ Provides instruction and practice in working with others to solve problems.

Communication Skills

6. _____ Develops communication skills, including active listening and the art of persuasion.

7. _____ Develops the ability and will to discuss current issues in a responsible (civil) manner.

Respect

8. _____ Encourages caring for others and service for the common good.

9. _____ Encourages understanding and appreciation for both diversity and unity.

Civic Engagement

10. _____ Contributes to the welfare of the school or broader community.

11. _____ Supports informed voting and democratic decision-making.

12. _____ Encourages advocacy of improved policy, laws, or procedures.

13. _____ Encourages action to secure more equitable civil and human rights.

_____ **Total Checks**

Civic Responsibility Meter Tool

Suggestions for use:

1. Ask students to reflect on what it means to be a good citizen in a democratic republic. Share and discuss the different perspectives that emerge. Then, compare the array of views with the thirteen Meter components and check for understanding of each of them.

2. Use the Meter as an initial planning resource. Review each of the thirteen components and then select the ones you want to include and emphasize in your service-learning project.

3. Use the Meter as a thirteen-lens instrument to analyze the civic education content of a service-learning project. This analysis could be done during the planning process for a project or after a project has been completed.

4. Ask students who have completed a service-learning project to use the Meter to reflect on how it impacted their civic skills, knowledge, and attitudes. Facilitate a conversation on ways to strengthen the civic education impact of the service-learning project next time for other students.

5. Ask students to select one or two Meter components for emphasis in their service-learning experience. Ask them to monitor and reflect on these components before, during, and after their experience.

6. Use the Meter to develop a benchmark for service-learning projects one year and then measure change over time as efforts are made to enhance the selected civic education components.

7. Pass out brief descriptions of four service-learning projects, either the ones included in this booklet, or descriptions that you create. Ask students or teachers to use the Meter to assess the civic responsibility in each of the projects individually. Then, provide time to discuss their assessments in small groups and report their judgments to the total group. Finally, facilitate a discussion about the different assessments to help clarify and deepen understanding of the meaning of civic responsibility and the potential to use it to enhance a service-learning project.

8. If there are multiple groups with service projects, they can use the Meter to help each other strengthen their plan. After a discussion of the components of the Civic Responsibility Meter, groups take turns as consultants for each other, listening to a presentation of the project and making suggestions on how it could be stronger in the components of civic responsibility.

Planning and Preparing for Success

Start your planning with your goals, and the goals of your students, in mind. What are your academic and civic learning goals? What goals do you have for the program, school, or district? How will you know if your project has reached your goals? What will you see, feel, or hear? What exactly will take place? What are the various tasks and assignments? What supplies, if any, are needed? Is there a sequence of tasks that need to occur over time?

These basic kinds of planning questions are an important part of preparation. The amount of planning needed will vary considerably by project. If students are going to a classroom of younger children for reading, for example, the planning would focus on scheduling and selecting books from the library. On the other hand, if students are helping a local organization refurbish homes to make them accessible for people with disabilities, the action will involve many steps, from getting permits and supplies to doing the remodeling in the appropriate order.

GETTING FROM AN IDEA TO A PROJECT

Step One: Determine Your Entry Point

Select your method for getting started and making curricular connections, beginning with an existing program or activity, specific content and skills, a unit of study, a student-identified need, or a community-identified need. Bear in mind the organizational context for your work and meet with potential community partners at this stage to define key elements of your project.

Step Two: Determine Where You Are Going

Define the academic, youth development, and community goals of your program and the context of your work. Clarify how you and students will know that they have mastered and demonstrated skills.

Step Three: Review the K–12 Service-Learning Standards for Quality Practice

This will remind you of what you need to keep in mind as you plan your project.

Step Four: Outline Your Plan

Develop a plan that includes all the elements of your project. Try to focus on three to five goals at most, including clear evidence of learning. You might use a curriculum-based process so the program will be more closely tied to your course content. Or, especially if you're part of a community-based organization, you might be more likely to use the project-based process and engage students more directly in all stages of the project development.

Step Five: Define the Roles of Your Partners

Make contacts with existing and potential partners—teachers, agency representatives, community volunteers, or others. Clarify the specific goals, roles, and responsibilities for all involved.

Step Six: Develop Your Plans and Gather Resources

Refine your plan based on learning that is most central to your context. Explore the best way for students to define the evidence of learning so they will understand clearly what mastery will look like. Use the checklist in this chapter to be sure you have considered logistical and safety issues. Some of this logistical planning can also be done later with students involved in both identifying the action that needs to be taken and taking responsibility for leadership. (You might find it helpful to have a colleague review your plan or check out websites listed below to see if other teachers' curricula might provide some helpful hints.)

Step Seven: Begin the Process of Service-Learning in Action

As you put your plan into action, explore ways to more effectively engage students and community partners.

Step Eight: Monitor and Continually Improve Design

Once the demonstration and the closing reflection have been completed, review and assess the learning, youth development, and community impacts against your original goals. Engage students and community partners in this assessment process. As you debrief, develop some specific plans for what you will do next time and explore ways to both sustain and deepen the quality of the projects. You might find it helpful to use the Standards of Practice Rubric as an element of your program review.

RESOURCES AND PLANNING ELEMENTS

Once you begin to plan out the details of a project, you'll find you have a wide variety of issues to consider. To keep the wealth of information at a manageable level, focus on these first:

People Resources

Service-learning experiences involve a variety of people, and the resources and needs they bring to the project will do much to shape it. Projects need to match the developmental abilities of the young people who participate, as well as the size of the group working together, the mix of skills they offer, and the needs of the service recipients. Think about whether or not you have community members who can help train young people or mentor them through specific components of a project. Are there existing efforts in your community that you and your students can build upon?

Financial Resources

Will you need funding to get students to a service site or purchase materials for the project? Will you need seeds for a garden, first aid kits, equipment or paint for a mural, additional supervisors, or rental space? Some of these needs can be met through volunteers or a loan of equipment. Never underestimate the power of students when asking for resources to support a project they believe in.

Logistical Resources

Service-learning projects can require careful logistical planning to make sure you have the time necessary to complete the project. How far in advance do you need to reserve school buses? Do you have clear maps to your sites and a safe place for buses to load and unload students? Do you have an extra map to give to your bus driver? Will you need parental permission, liability and medical releases, name tags, and substitutes? What capacity does your school have to provide this kind of support? Will you need to be solely responsible for logistics planning, or can your students take on many of those tasks?

PREPARING STUDENTS FOR SERVICE-LEARNING

When embarking on a new service-learning project, it's important to consider things from the perspective of students. They need to be prepared for the project, even if it's something that seems relatively simple, and given enough instruction and information to feel confident.

Orientation to the Service

If students are doing research or presentations, make sure they understand any guidelines that should define their work. What standards are being set by the community? What support will they have and who is the beneficiary of their work? If students will be doing physical work, they need to know what to wear, what supplies to bring, how to handle the equipment they will use, and so on. If students are expected to use gloves or wear rain gear, do not assume they will remember to bring the gear. Have some extras on hand. It's also a good idea to introduce them to any terms or concepts they might hear or use. A quick introductory session with a professional in the field they'll be working in can reduce the confusion and insecurity they might feel later on.

Skills Building

Whether or not young people need to develop certain physical skills, there will likely be some interpersonal skills they will need to master. As comfortable as they may be talking with people they know well, they may not know how to initiate a conversation with an elderly person in a care facility, a government official, or others they encounter whose language or lifestyle seems very different from their own.

Knowing whom they are likely to meet in the course of the service project, and having some conversation starters ready, can make the experience much easier. They may also need some direction on what questions not to ask or not to answer. Let students practice their new skills through some spirited role-playing in pairs or small groups.

In addition, don't assume that young people understand appropriate conduct and etiquette in the setting in which they will serve. Consider addressing the following questions:

- What etiquette skills do the students need to have? If possible, role-play potential situations.

- How do people in the setting and those being served prefer to be addressed?

- If you're working with another agency, does it have specific rules or regulations students need to be aware of?

- Are there cultural differences in terms of dress, language, gestures, or other customs that are important for students to understand?

- What kind of clothing is most appropriate for the service site so students are comfortable and can easily establish rapport?

Orientation to Different People and Environments

One of the rich opportunities in service-learning is for young people to have experiences in different settings or cultures. Preparing them in advance with information and opportunities to practice skills can nurture in them the confidence they need to deal with these new and sometimes intimidating situations. Details about what they will do should be balanced with information about what they might see or feel.

The students will want to know what the site is like, what they are likely to encounter there, and whether or not they will be safe. The more they know about the site, the less orientation they'll need later on. An advance tour of the site can be a great way to accomplish this, although photos or videos can also be helpful if a tour is not practical.

If young people will be working in an organization or agency, make sure they understand the agency's mission, history, and program. If possible, introduce them to key people in the program ahead of time.

PREPARING ADULT PARTNERS FOR SERVICE-LEARNING

In the same way that your students need to be prepared for service-learning, the community partners and other adults who will work with them also need to be ready for the experience of working with young people. In many cases the adult allies and partners benefit from participating in the same training and orientation as the young people—not just to prepare them, but also to build relationships and shared experiences with the students.

Preparing adults might involve exploring such questions as:

- How will we each work to create supportive, caring relationships with the young people?
- How will we ensure that all the young people feel they are valued and contributing?
- How will the adults explicating teach or reinforce the academic, civic, or leadership skills?
- How will adults help students understand the context and purpose of their community work?
- How will adults help students see connections to various career pathways?
- What is our role in setting and enforcing boundaries?
- How will we help young people develop their own skills, values, and commitments?
- What skills do we have that we can help nurture in young people?
- How will they help young people understand future opportunities for service, volunteering, and leadership at their community site?

If your students will be working in a setting that hasn't engaged young people before, it's important to talk ahead of time about appropriate ways to interact with and support young people. Too often community partners can have preconceptions about young people that interfere with the students' ability to contribute and learn.

Engaging Parents

Parents can be important allies in your service-learning efforts—or they can be obstacles if they have many unanswered questions. They need to know what's going to happen, why it is important to do, what their children are intended to learn, and how they can be supportive and involved.

Depending on the service-learning project you are doing, there are many ways to engage parents. If the project is short-term and local, you may want to only inform parents about it and get permission for their children to participate. If, however, the project is longer, out of town, or has higher demands, you will want to find a way to disseminate information, identify specific ways parents can participate and support the project, and give parents a forum for asking questions.

SAFEGUARDS AND LIABILITY

Any educational program, particularly those involving young people, contains an element of risk. Service-learning challenges are no different from those of athletic teams, work experience programs, or field trips that take students out into the community. And many of the policies and release forms for those programs can either be used as is or adapted for community activities that are part of a service-learning program.

Risk management is an important component of service-learning that encourages or requires students to work with the community. Thoughtfully developed policies and procedures can help teachers and administrators manage risks effectively. Because "documents of agreement," which attempt to reduce and/or transfer responsibility for harm are governed by state law, it is good practice to review written consent and/or liability forms with the administration's risk manager or legal counsel.

Work-study policies that guide off-site career placements can be applied to independent service-learning programs as well. The following recommendations should guide programs that involve a large number of students in service-learning:

1. Utilize the school district's risk management professionals and/or legal department to review policies, procedures, and forms, and articulate and publish service-learning policies, procedures, goals, and benefits for students, parents, staff, agencies, and service recipients. Be sure to adjust and modify as needed.

2. Identify risks and liabilities; develop policies, procedures, and training for students and staff; and develop goals, objectives, and curriculum for the community project.

3. Require parental/guardian permission (in writing) for student involvement. The permission form needs to thoroughly describe the community activity and any potential dangers.

4. Become familiar with child labor laws and Labor and Industry standards to ensure that students are not engaging in prohibited activities. (For example, students may not use power tools; youth must be adequately trained for any on-site tasks.) For more information on federal law, contact the U.S. Department of Labor (dol.gov).

5. Be sure there are supervisors at each service placement site.

6. Develop training and handbooks that cover health, safety, and emergency crisis plans. Training should include information about inherent risks. Include this information in the student handbook and service site procedures handbook.

7. Be sure transportation policies for students traveling to and from the service-learning site follow all school district requirements and state laws governing student drivers and school transportation safety laws.

8. Students traveling off campus during school hours should have medical release forms available on site.

9. Student medical and mental conditions that might impact the students' safety or abilities must be known by students, the community coordinator, and the school coordinator.

Good judgment and common sense often dictate what is safe and appropriate activity. What is safe in one set of circumstances may not be classified as safe in another set of circumstances. For example, changing weather conditions call for you to assess a situation and possibly discontinue an activity. If you are uncertain about the safety of an activity, give the district full details and don't proceed without district approval.

The safety of the students is your most important consideration. Because of their youth and inexperience, children need guidance and support from adults. Adults must determine the degree of care required according to the child's age and skill and the nature of the activity. Err on the side of caution when considering whether to proceed with an activity.

SOME BASIC PLANNING GUIDELINES

In addition to the above safety guidelines, the following recommendations can help you plan your service-learning project.

1. Require all participants to wear identification badges and to sign in and out with each visit. Student ID cards are helpful when placing students out in the community.

2. Provide adult supervision based on your district's field trip adult-student ratio (1 adult/8 students). Some districts may allow parents, substitutes, and Ameri-Corps or community volunteers to help provide supervision. Any adults who are supervising students alone must have successfully completed background checks or fingerprinting.

3. Include health, safety, first aid, and emergency crisis plans in project orientation.

4. Require that the teacher or service sites have a first aid kit, copies of the student's medical release form, and clear instructions on what to do if the student is injured.

Student Orientation

At the community site students should be instructed to

- Never do anything they have not been trained to do.
- Follow their gut instinct if they are uncomfortable, and get help.
- Ask questions.
- Never use power tools.
- Find out where they can get help if they need it.
- Know emergency exits and procedures.
- Understand the educational purpose, expectations, and value of the service-learning project.

Parent Orientation

Parents should

- Thoroughly understand the purpose of the service-learning program and expectations of the service-learning project.

Service Project Safety Review

The following questions can help you set up a safe service-learning experience.

Supervision

- Are students supervised at all times?
- If there are adults who will supervise the students alone, have they completed a background check?

Adequate Training

- What training will be necessary to complete the project well and safely?
- Who is best able to provide that training?
- What equipment is necessary for all students to be actively engaged in the project? Most states prohibit the use of power machinery by students under the age of 18.
- Who will provide this equipment?
- How can we best prepare students with the specific skills they will need to complete their work?

Medical Care

- Who will have a first aid kit and who will have medical releases in case of emergency?
- Do students need any special clothing?
- Are on-site supervisors informed of any medical allergies or concerns?
- Do on-site supervisors have access to medical release forms in case of an emergency?

Overall Safety

- Are there any safety issues related to transportation that you need to prepare for?
- Is a cell phone needed in case of an emergency? If so, who will provide it?
- If any participants are under 18, have you provided parents with an accurate description of the project, and have they signed a release indicating that they are aware of any risks involved and authorize their child's participation?
- If students are working on a community site during the school day without direct teacher supervision they need to have medical/accident insurance. Be sure the school is informed of any accidents and district accident reports are filled out.

- Inform the school supervisor of their child's unique health and behavior needs.

- Provide adequate medical accident insurance. If they don't have insurance, they can usually purchase health coverage for their child through the school. Some examples include Excel Serve, PTSA Student Accident Insurance, and L and I Volunteer Insurance.

- Review the information sent home regarding the project site and activities and sign off only if they are comfortable with the value and safety of the project.

- Provide their child with appropriate clothing and equipment for activities, or contact the leader before the activity to find sources for the necessary clothing and equipment.

- Assist the leaders when their child has special needs or disabilities.

- Make provisions for their children to get to or from meeting places in a timely manner.

Teacher/Supervisor Orientation

Educators should

- Conduct a hazard mapping of the site prior to the service activity.

- Make sure there is not unsupervised access to children.

- Be sure your students are supervised if they have direct contact with agency clients. (If students will be regularly working with children and the elderly, background checks should be completed on the student volunteers.)

- Be sure all parties (student, parent, and community members) understand the educational purpose, expectations, and process of the service-learning project.

- Partner with law enforcement to provide background checks and, if necessary, fingerprinting for community and parent supervisors.

- Be sure students are adequately trained prior to the service-learning projects so they know how to safely complete their tasks and how to respond in case of emergency.

- Create a statement of social, emotional, and physical barriers to student success for parents to complete regarding their child (i.e., need-to-know information).

Service Site

Community agencies should

- Develop a learning plan for participating students.

- Offer or provide volunteer insurance.

- Have adults who are working unsupervised with students complete a background check.

- Inform students of safety and emergency procedures before students begin working on their service activities. Model safe behaviors and provide time to respond to questions and concerns.

Background Checks

This is required for all adults who will have unsupervised access to children, developmentally disabled persons, or vulnerable adults. You may choose to use State Patrol information. It is your responsibility to ensure that background checks comply with the policies of the agencies and schools.

Further resource and program examples can be found at projectserviceleadership.org in the Learn, Serve, Succeed section.

RESOURCES

The Complete Guide to Service Learning: Proven, Practical Ways to Engage Students in Civic Responsibility, Academic Curriculum, and Social Action by Cathryn Berger Kaye, Free Spirit Publishing. A comprehensive guide to all aspects of planning and implementing service-learning projects, this book provides background information about service-learning and current standards of practice, ideas for projects related to a variety of issues (the environment, the elderly, social justice), and a bookshelf of literature related to community issues.

K–12 Service-Learning Project Planning Toolkit from RMC Research Corporation National Service-Learning Clearinghouse, 2009. The materials in this toolkit contain information about the five core components of a service-learning project: investigation, planning and preparation, the service activity, reflection, and demonstration/celebration. Also included are the K–12 Service-Learning Standards for Quality Practice. At servicelearning.org/filemanager/download/8542_K-12_SL_Toolkit_UPDATED.pdf.

The National Service Learning Clearinghouse is a resource for service-learning research, manuals, and service-learning units. At servicelearning.org.

Youth Service America provides manuals on various issues and tips sheets on a wide variety of topics. The "Semester of Service Strategy Guide" is filled with wonderful tips and planning tools. YSA also sponsors a variety of service-learning grants for teachers. At ysa.org.

Culminating Project Resources and Guidelines has a variety of tools that help teachers and districts more effectively plan their senior/culminating projects so they are meaningful to the community and to students. The site includes project rubrics, planning guides, and tip sheets for parents and community agencies. At projectserviceleadership .org/culminatingprojects.

Logistical Planning Checklist

☐ **Clarify Where Your Project Will Take Place**

- Do you have permission to use the space?
- Is there a fee?
- Do you have limited time at the project area?

☐ **Investigate Transportation Sources**

- What kind of transportation might you need?
- How much will it cost?
- How many people need transportation?

☐ **Consider Supplying Refreshments**

- Will you be supplying any food or drink during the project?
- What will you need? How often?
- How much will it cost?
- Can you get some or all of the refreshments donated?

☐ **Gather Project Materials**

- What project materials will you need? Make a very specific list.
- How much will materials cost?
- Can you get any of the items donated?
- Can you use recycled supplies?

☐ **Plan Project Orientation**

- Who will orient students to the site and project?
- Who will orient partners?
- Are etiquette and cultural orientation needed?
- What skills do students need to acquire?
- What background information is still needed?

☐ **Plan for Safety Issues**

- Have you checked the site for appropriateness and safety for students?
- Have you obtained parent permission forms?
- Do you need additional insurance?
- Are medical release forms required?

☐ **Engage Partners**

- Who will help supervise students?
- How will the community partner help students understand the value and context of their service?
- What family members or community members can you involve? How will you ask them to participate?
- What type and frequency of communication with each partner is needed?
- What will you do to prepare participants for the project? Can you provide speakers? Offer activities? Present videos?
- How will you validate the value of the service provided?

☐ **Develop a Publicity Plan**

- How will you present your project? Who will you present it to?
- What media avenues can you use?
- Will some media outlets donate publicity time, like radio and TV stations, newspapers, or other publications?

☐ **Create a Budget**

- How much do you anticipate your service-learning project will cost?
- Can you define where all the costs will come from?
- Who can help with funds in the event of unforeseen problems?

Service-Learning Participants and Roles

Use this chart to record the many people and groups who will participate in your service-learning project. Think about the roles they will fill. How were they involved in planning the service-learning project, and how will you communicate with them about results?

PARTICIPANTS	ROLE	HOW ARE THEY INVOLVED IN PROJECT PLANNING?	HOW WILL YOU COMMUNICATE WITH THEM?
Students			
Classroom teacher			
Parents			
Community partner (community agencies, government, local businesses, etc.)			
Community partner			
Service recipients			
Media			

Service-Learning Planning Tool

School: _____

Teacher(s): _____

Community partner(s): _____

Purpose
Why are you developing a service-learning project? How will students benefit? What community need(s) will be addressed?

Standards
What standards will be met?

Civic Skills
What civic skills, attributes, or knowledge will be fostered through this experience?

- ☐ Understanding of community resources and organizations
- ☐ Awareness of community issues
- ☐ Ability to identify personal values and beliefs about an issue
- ☐ Ability to use logical argument to support values and beliefs
- ☐ Ability to understand the root causes of issues
- ☐ Ability to connect community issue and academic coursework
- ☐ Awareness that students themselves are a strong resource within the community
- ☐ Other

Career-Related/Life Skills
What career-related skills, attributes, or knowledge will be fostered through this experience?

- ☐ Critical-thinking and problem-solving skills
- ☐ Ability to work as part of a team
- ☐ Ability to assume different group roles
- ☐ Increased performance as self-directed and active learners
- ☐ Heightened self-esteem
- ☐ Ability to take pride in success
- ☐ Other

Community Impact and Involvement
How will the product or service be of value to the greater community?

- ☐ Develops positive school-community relationships
- ☐ Addresses a stated community need
- ☐ Helps individuals meet basic needs
- ☐ Creates public awareness of important issues
- ☐ Offers valuable information to the greater community
- ☐ Gives a voice to marginalized groups
- ☐ Provides community members with new opportunities to learn
- ☐ Creates an opportunity for community members to feel valued
- ☐ Other

How will you maximize the role and resources of the community?

☐ Communicate with community partner consistently throughout service-learning experience

☐ Design project goals and expectations in collaboration with community partner

☐ Identify program needs and determine ways the community can support students

☐ Involve community partners in reflection and debriefing sessions

☐ Provide opportunities for community to assess student work

☐ Invite community partners to school for celebration activities

☐ Other

Design and Implementation

Preparation

• What knowledge or skills must students attain before being able to master core academic skills of the service-learning project?

Content knowledge:

Skills:

• What preparation will you provide for the community partner so it can engage students and maximize student learning?

Ownership and Engagement

How will students be involved in the design and implementation of the project? We will

☐ Provide students a core subject area and encourage them to generate project ideas.

☐ Give students a list of project ideas to select from.

☐ Identify the project and ask students for implementation ideas.

☐ Ask students to contact organizations to inquire about community needs.

☐ Brainstorm community needs and explore potential projects based on these needs.

☐ Design project goals and expectations in collaboration with students.

☐ Encourage students to assume various roles throughout the service-learning experience.

☐ Other

Reflection

What reflection activities will be included in this service-learning experience?

☐ Regular verbal check-in

☐ Personal journal

☐ Pair-sharing

☐ Chalk talk

☐ Regular written reflection

☐ Group discussion

☐ Debrief sessions with community partners

☐ Other

How will you help students see connections between course objectives and the service-learning project?

Materials and Resources

• What educational materials will students use?

• What resources, transportation, supplies, and/or equipment will students need to accomplish the objectives?

Action Plan
What needs to be done? Who is responsible? When is it needed?

1.

2.

3.

4.

5.

6.

7.

8.

Evaluation:

How will the impact on the community be assessed?

☐ Verbal check-in

☐ Survey/questionnaire

☐ Observation

☐ Roundtable with community partner

☐ Written reflection

☐ Group discussion

☐ Observation and analysis

☐ Quality of product

☐ Other

How will student learning be assessed?

☐ Subject-area testing

☐ Student reflection on learning

☐ Observation

☐ Roundtable with community partner

☐ Core concept quiz

☐ Group discussion

☐ Checklist/rubric

☐ Review/evaluation of product

☐ Other

How will success be celebrated?

☐ Verbal praise

☐ Public exhibition

☐ Peer acknowledgment

☐ Post pictures/reflections on bulletin board

☐ Awards

☐ Community acknowledgment

☐ Submit article to district/school newsletter

☐ Celebration day

☐ Other

How will you let others know?
(media, district, school, parents, etc.)

☐ Write a press release

☐ Submit article to district/school newsletter

☐ Invite parents/guardians to class presentations

☐ Make announcement at school event

☐ Send photos to local newspaper

☐ Invite students, staff, and parents to project preview

☐ Encourage students to present project at district meeting

☐ Post pictures/reflections on bulletin board

☐ Other

This tool was developed by CESNW coach Kate McPherson and adapted by Angela Nusom, a teacher at Centennial Learning Center, 2006.

Establishing Evidence of Learning

How will you know if students are achieving the **learning goals** you've identified for their service-learning projects?

What academic **standards** and **benchmarks** will be met as students plan and provide the service activities?

What **civic goals** will the project address? What civic knowledge, skills (e.g., informed decision-making, listening, expressing their opinions), and dispositions (e.g., tolerance, sense of responsibility for others, believing they can make a difference in the world) will be developed?

What **other learning** do you hope students will gain from the project (e.g., social skills, career exploration, learning to manage conflict, and/or learning about themselves)?

Are youth developing the ability to apply what they are learning to **new contexts**?

Will students develop **analytical** and **creative thinking** skills?

As schools and community organizations increasingly focus on helping students master core academic skills and support high school completion while developing student problem-solving, civic, leadership, and work-readiness skills, service-learning programs have the unique opportunity to provide rich, experiential ways to enable students to both acquire and demonstrate learning. However, if students (along with teachers and administrators) do not have clear evidence that they have achieved these academic standards, teachers may find that even the most engaging service-learning programs may be called into question. Of course, students may not recognize their own learning.

Enabling students to clearly demonstrate their learning at high levels of proficiency will help both school- and community-based service-learning thrive, and, more importantly, it will help students have ways to measure their own mastery—celebrating their success and calibrating their need to learn more.

Taking time to establish clear and rigorous performance targets for students will enable more of them to master important skills and know they have mastered them. In addition, service-learning programs will have clear evidence that participants are learning.

EVIDENCE OF LEARNING

Developing an effective way to guide and assess high academic standards takes time and thoughtful planning. There is a wide variety of ways to assess targeted learning goals. As educators develop methods to assess student learning, they can certainly start with the kinds of activities they have used in the past—tests, surveys, essays, etc. Even if a teacher uses a performance rubric to guide and assess the application of skills, there is no reason to start from scratch. There are many instruments that have been developed and refined by teachers.

The material in this chapter can also assist both schools and community-based organizations in developing ways for students to demonstrate mastery and increase the possibility for students to receive academic credit through their service-learning programs. While it takes time to learn about content standards, learning assessment, and credit granting, this may be time well invested if we hope to work together on behalf of student graduation and success in life.

Note to community-based educators: While these tools are predominately used in classroom settings, community-based service-learning programs can more intentionally support academic learning and become stronger allies with schools if they become more proficient in their assessment of academic learning. This may also help more students finally master the skills that have seemed confusing or irrelevant in the classroom. At the same time, community-based organizations should take care that their efforts to measure academic achievement do not lead them to become too school-like, or they may become less welcoming for many youth.

ASSESSMENT STRATEGIES

To guide and evaluate student learning, teachers need to develop clear assessment strategies. The chart below (developed by Rick Stiggins, Assessment Training Institute, Inc.) can help teachers select the assessment method that best matches student learning goals.[1]

One of the unique opportunities and challenges of service-learning is that such experiential projects allow multiple opportunities for students to acquire knowledge, practice skills, and demonstrate how they've increased their capabilities. Each step of the service-learning process provides opportunities for process skills (project planning, civic problem solving, scientific process, teamwork), not just subject-matter knowledge students acquire.

Assessment Methods That Match Student Learning Goals

	SELECTED RESPONSE	WRITTEN RESPONSE	PERFORMANCE ASSESSMENT	PERSONAL COMMUNICATION
KNOWLEDGE	**Good** Can assess isolated elements of knowledge and some relationships among them	**Strong** Can assess elements of knowledge and relationships among them	**Partial** Can assess elements of knowledge and relationships among them in certain contexts	**Strong** Can assess elements of knowledge and relationships among them
REASONING	**Good** Can assess many but not all reasoning targets	**Strong** Can assess all reasoning targets	**Partial** Can assess reasoning targets in the context of certain tasks in certain contexts	**Strong** Can assess all reasoning targets
SKILL	**Poor** Cannot assess skill level; can only assess prerequisite knowledge and reasoning	**Poor** Cannot assess skill level; can only assess prerequisite knowledge and reasoning	**Strong** Can observe and assess skills as they are being performed	**Partial** Strong match for some oral communication proficiencies; not a good match otherwise
PRODUCT	**Poor** Cannot assess the quality of a product; can only assess prerequisite knowledge and reasoning	**Poor** Cannot assess the quality of a product; can only assess prerequisite knowledge and reasoning	**Strong** Can directly assess the attributes of quality of products	**Poor** Cannot assess the quality of a product; can only assess prerequisite knowledge and reasoning

Although service-learning is similar to other active learning methods—such as project-based, problem-based, inquiry-based, and work-based learning—what is unique in its other approaches is the use of community service as the active learning vehicle. Service-learning simultaneously enhances students' academic, civic, social, and personal development. The broad application of service-learning and the multiple education purposes it serves have implications not only for how service-learning is organized and implemented but also how students' learning is assessed.

HELPFUL TIPS FROM THE FIELD

This chapter is filled with examples of tools teachers have developed or used to guide and assess student academic and process skills. They have the following suggestions to pass on to school and community educators.

1. Focus your assessment on a few primary goals: one to three academic content standards and one or two process skills. If you assess too many goals it becomes complicated for both you and your students. Also, the assessment can take away from the energy of the project.

2. Blend your methods of assessment (written responses, surveys, rubrics, tests, etc.).

3. Be sure you establish very specific indicators of success. Creating a rubric with students can ensure that students are very clear about what the indicators of success are and what your expectations are.

4. Work with students to establish high expectations of thinking and action. This will help everyone understand the importance of the work.

5. To more completely assess what students are learning through service-learning, assessment needs to include students' gains in knowledge and understanding about important social issues as well as the development of specific civic action skills. For example, as students gather data for a water quality project, what have they learned about the importance of water quality? What have they come to understand about how nonprofits, government, business, and individual volunteers are working together to have an impact on this issue at a local, state, or national level? What have they learned about working as a team to organize the information they have gathered, and how have they determined who needs to hear what they have learned, and why? What have they learned about community problem solving?

THE PROCESS

The following process can be used to engage students in developing student-friendly evidence of their learning. Students are often more demanding of themselves as they determine how they will know that they have really learned something and can use their skills to actually do something. Involving them in the process also ensures that they are more likely to understand what success will look like when they have achieved it.

After identifying the broad parameters of your project, you have the opportunity to engage students in linking specific academic objectives to their planned service and identifying the actions required to meet both their service and learning goals, and they can be your partners in assessing how well their goals are being met.

Note: Principles of backward design, as outlined in Understanding by Design by Jay McTighe and Grant Wiggins, can be especially helpful when planning assessment and evaluation for service-learning projects (grantwiggins.org/ubd/ubd.lasso).

Pre-Service

- Share the content standards and desired learning outcomes, as well as the service goals, with students so they know what's expected of them.

- Post and review the questions they will explore during the service-learning project as they are planning what they will do.

- Elicit students' help in listing the important knowledge and skills students will learn during their project.

During Service

- At the start of the project, talk with the students about the types of assessments they'll participate in to show evidence of learning and understanding by the end of the project. What products, performances, and other evidence will you assess? What parts of their work will be assessed individually and what will be evaluated as a group?

- Share the culminating performance tasks and accompanying rubrics so students will know what will be expected and how their work will be judged.

- Whenever possible, show examples of student work on similar tasks so students can see what quality looks like.

Post-Service

- Explicitly connect the learning experiences and direct instruction during the service-learning project with the desired results, essential questions, and expected performances.

- Have students regularly reflect on what they are learning and how it will help them with their tasks in the service-learning project as well as in life and other areas of school.

If done well, making the learning process more transparent can also empower students; they will be able to take increasing responsibility of their learning because they will often see learning as a process—identifying a learning goal, developing a project/process that will teach or demonstrate the skill/content, and demonstrating mastery. Most students experience their education as passengers, simply following the steps laid out by a teacher. It can be eye-opening for them to explore ways they can become the driver of their own education.

Below are a few examples of service-learning projects that have clear student learning goals and aligned assessment activities.

Cross-Age Teaching

Kids Care students learn by teaching. The self-contained core class of seventh and eighth graders is trained to tutor younger students in reading. They spend two days a week tutoring in elementary schools. Data dispel any doubt that Kids Care is effective for tutees and tutors alike. As proud as Discovery Middle School is of the data, it is the day-to-day observations that show just how much the Kids Care program works for these middle schoolers. Elementary students who were tutored showed great gains in reading, also. With younger students looking up to them, the middle schoolers see themselves as role models. When they help others learn to read, they see themselves as readers. They believed the honor roll was an attainable, personal goal. Teachers noticed improved behavior, and attendance soared.

Statistics tell the story of success:

- *The Kids Care core class had a total of 52 students.*

- *20 of the 52 were eligible for Title services (38 percent).*

- *On tutoring days, an average of only 2 students out of the 52 were absent, with periods of two weeks at a time with no one absent.*

- *As a core, students' GPA went up +1.0, on average, from the first trimester to the second.*

Academic Learning Requirements

Students must be able to

- *Use word recognition and word meaning skills to read and comprehend text.*
- *Comprehend important ideas and details.*
- *Set goals and evaluate progress to improve reading.*
- *Assess strengths and need for improvement.*
- *Seek and offer feedback to improve reading.*
- *Develop interests and share reading experiences.*

Assessment

- *A standard reading-levels test is given to gauge overall reading level.*
- *A miscue analysis test is given before, during, and after the tutoring program, enabling the teacher to identify specific reading sub skills.*
- *Teacher observations determine the student's reading comfort level.*
- *Reading logs determine the volume and level of difficulty of the student's reading.*

Water Quality and Habitat Data Collection

Teacher Karen Lippy, North Mason High School in Washington, assessed the scientific knowledge students acquired as they conducted research on the tide water quality in Puget Sound, collected and managed data, and reported the data to the Department of Ecology.

Academic Learning Requirements

Students must be able to

- *Understand and describe the characteristics, structure, and functions of organisms.*
- *Use information, skills, and investigative processes employed in a field of science.*
- *Understand energy, its transformations, and interactions with matter.*
- *Explain and analyze the interaction of energy and matter.*
- *Conduct procedures to collect, organize, and display scientific data to facilitate scientific analysis and interpretation.*

Assessment

- *Essay questions substantiate content knowledge.*
- *Given pictures and descriptions of organisms with a food web, students arrange them in their trophic levels (producer and various consumer levels).*
- *Students identify the energy source and direction energy travels, and label any scavengers or decomposers. Students describe the effects of the forces of the sun, moon, and centrifugal forces on ocean tides.*

- *Students demonstrate their ability to apply scientific problem-solving by performing tasks (such as predict the correct time and tide height for a given location when given appropriate tide tables).*
- *Students demonstrate their ability to collect and interpret data by completing a scientific report.*

Letter to the Editor

Students in computer application class learn the skills of writing and formatting business letters. Marilyn Dale-Bourke puts more punch into this class by encouraging students to write letters to public officials or newspapers regarding issues they care about. Students learn the components of persuasive, bad news, and good news business letters and compose individual examples. They also compose a letter to the editor of their local or school newspaper.

Academic Learning Requirements
Students must be able to

- *Write clearly and effectively.*
- *Write in a variety of forms for different audiences and purposes.*
- *Understand and use the steps of the writing process.*
- *Communicate ideas clearly and effectively.*
- *Read different materials for a variety of purposes.*

Assessment

- *Students compose a letter to the editor of their local or school newspaper.*
- *They will identify one to three issues to discuss, then state their position clearly with factual support.*
- *For each "problem" identified, the student must offer at least one suggestion for improvement.*

For more information on this topic, see "Service-Learning: Progress Monitoring, Assessment, and Evaluation" by Lawrence Neil Bailis and Kate McPherson at search-institute .org/about/learn-serve-succeed.

Further resource and program examples can be found at projectserviceleadership.org in the Learn, Serve, Succeed section.

RESOURCES

The Buck Institute has great resources on development tools and activities that can be used to assess student learning. These tools are exceptionally helpful for project-based learning. At bie.org.

Principles of backward design as outlined in ***Understanding by Design*** by Jay McTighe and Grant Wiggins can be especially helpful when planning assessment and evaluation for service-learning projects. At grantwiggins.org/ubd/ubd.lasso.

Pearson Assessment Training Institute (ATI) helps teachers improve student achievement by integrating student-involved classroom assessment into day-to-day instruction. At assessmentinst.com.

NOTE

1. R. Stiggins, "Developing a Total Quality Assessment Environment," Portland, OR: Assessment Training Institute, 1995.

Predicting Evidence of Learning: A Planning Process

Use this form to record your learning goal and connect that goal to academic standards or benchmarks. Then predict what you will see from your students and how they will demonstrate their learning, noting possible assessment tools.

Learning Goals

Content standards (math, science, history, civics, writing, reading, oral communication)

Work readiness skills (team skills, resume writing, interviewing, time management, collaboration)

Civic skills/predispositions (understand community sectors, civic decision-making)

Service goals/community impacts (habitat restored, increased understanding of civic and individual responsibility for habitat preservation, understanding of policies that pertain to civic issues)

Academic Standards or Benchmarks Related to These Goals

Questions Students Will Explore

Assessment Evidence Linked to These Goals, Standards, and Questions

PERFORMANCE TASKS	PRODUCTS	DOCUMENTATION

Reflection, Demonstration, and Celebration

Much of what we learn in life comes from reflecting on our experiences. Guided reflection helps students generate connections between their service-learning experiences, academic content, and career-related learning goals.

Experience has shown that reflection is most effective when:

- It is done before, during, and after the service activities.

- It is well organized, intentional, and continuous.

- It involves the community partners. Some of the most compelling reflection activities actively involve people who are receiving the service as well as the students who are doing the service.

- It utilizes a variety of learning styles.

PRE-SERVICE REFLECTION

Set the stage for service-learning by helping students understand the purpose and the context for their community service experience. Having students reflect on previous service experiences can help them learn from the past to develop future plans for success. To help students, ask questions like:

- What service activities have you done in the past?

- In what ways was this service experience effective for you and the community? In what ways was it not valuable?

- As you prepare for your service activities, what can you learn from that experience that might help you be more effective in future service activities?

PRE-SERVICE REFLECTION ACTIVITIES

A Know-Want-Learn Chart

Have students complete a Know-Want-Learn (KWL) chart. Make a chart showing what you know (K) and what you want to know (W), and when you complete your project, finish your chart with (L), what you learned.

K—What I know	W—What I want to know	L—What I learned

Poster Presentations

Ask students to make a poster that describes the issue they are working on and information about the organization they are going to be working with.

Photo Response

Have students look at a photo of the project site. Have them write what they know about the issue, based on their current knowledge.

Knowledge/Assumptions Inventory

Brainstorm what students know about an issue and record their answers on newsprint, or ask students to write down, anonymously, stereotypes they have related to the project. At the end of the project, revisit the students' reflections and discuss based on their experience at the service site.

Community Mapping

Design an activity in which participants walk or drive through a particular neighborhood or section of town and make observations about livability, income distribution, environmental health, or other relevant concepts by mapping the types of businesses, people, or graffiti they see during their "tour."

Two Voices Exercise

Find diverse perspectives related to your service project (from the newspaper, magazine, Internet, etc.). Recruit students to read two or more diverse perspectives on an issue. Ask the group: *Which position is most convincing to you? Why? How would these people justify their position? What further questions would you ask of these people if they were here with us? What voices are missing? What points are left out in these statements?*

Force Field Analysis

At the end of a community mapping activity, ask students to map out the positive and negative factors affecting livability or a related concept in a community. Ask: *Where does the balance lie? What would need to change in order for livability to be realized?*

POST-SERVICE REFLECTION

Use the following questions to design activities that help students reflect on their service project/experiences. (Modify the questions based on the grade/age of the student you are working with.) Be creative in how you use the questions! Use them to lead a class discussion, as journal prompts, or for an artistic activity.

What?

- Report what happened, objectively. Without judgment or interpretation, describe in detail the facts and events of the service experience. What happened? What is the issue you addressed? What events or "critical incidents" occurred?

- In what ways are you learning, applying, or demonstrating your career-related learning goals or your core academics?

- What careers and job were present at your service-learning site? What skills did employees use at their jobs? What training and education would adequately prepare someone for this work?

- How did you use your math, science, communication skills, etc.?

So What?

- Describe what was learned and what difference the event made.

- Discuss your feelings, ideas, and analysis of the service-learning experience.

- How is your experience different from what you expected?

- How have you affirmed or altered your previously assumed knowledge?

- What did you learn from the community that you served?

- What are some of the pressing issues in the community?

Now What?

- Brainstorm what you will do differently in the future as a result of the experience.

- How have these experiences shaped or affirmed your future plans as a learner, citizen, or worker?

- Consider broader implications of the service experience and apply learning.

- How is this experience tied to the community?

- What information can you share with your peers?

- What more would you like to learn about this issue?

- What larger social issues come to mind?

TIPS FOR SUCCESS

- Before you select a reflection activity, ask what you want your students to achieve through reflection and how the reflection connects to the primary learning goals of the project.

- Using a variety of reflective activities enables students to discover a method that suits their style.

- Reflection is a time to gather information, dispel stereotypes, and discuss frustrations, as well as celebrate.

- Be sure to wait after asking a question to allow enough time for people to process their experiences and build learning connections.

- Facilitators need to guide the discussion so the conversations stay focused and purposeful.

JOURNALS

While students often use journals to reflect upon their service-learning experiences, they often merely describe events at the community site. Journals can be an effective way to develop self-understanding and strengthen intrapersonal skills. Journals can also be a way to collect personal data during the project to be summarized in a more formal reflective paper near the end of the service-learning project.

Journal Options

Dialogue journal: Students submit loose-leaf pages or electronic documents bi-weekly for the teacher to read and comment on. While labor intensive for the instructor, this can provide continual feedback to students and prompt new questions for students to consider during the semester. Dialogue journals could also be read by a peer.

Double-entry journal: When using a double-entry journal, students are asked to write two one-page entries each week: students describe their personal thoughts and reactions to the service experience on the left page of the journal, and write about key issues from class discussion or readings on the right page of the journal. Students then draw arrows indicating relationships between their personal experience and service project.

Critical incident journal: This type of journal entry focuses the student on analysis of a particular event that occurred during the week. By answering one of the following sets of prompts, students are asked to consider their thoughts and reactions and articulate the action they plan to take in the future: *Describe a significant event that occurred as part of the service experience. Why was this significant to you? What underlying issues (career-related learning connection, societal, interpersonal, curricular) surfaced as a result of this experience? How will this incident influence your future behavior?* Another set of questions for a critical incident journal includes the following prompts: *Describe an incident or situation that created a dilemma for you in terms of what to say or do. What's the first thing you thought of to say or do? List three other actions you might have taken. Which of these actions seems best to you now and why do you think this is the best response?*

Three-part journal: Students are asked to divide each page of their journal into thirds and write weekly entries during their service project. In the top section, students describe some aspect of the service experience. In the middle of the page, they are asked to analyze how classroom learning relates to their service experience. In the third part of their page, students comment on how the experience and classroom learning can be applied to their personal or future work life.

QUESTIONS FOR DISCUSSIONS, ESSAYS, OR JOURNAL ENTRIES

The following questions make great conversation starters and essay or journal topics. Divided into subject groupings, teachers and youth workers can use them to jumpstart student thinking and reflection.

Careers

- What career pathway interests you, and why is it interesting to you?
- How did you develop or demonstrate career-related learning skills at your community site?
- What careers are present at the community site? What would be satisfying or frustrating about this job? What training would you need in order to be prepared for jobs in this field?
- What jobs do you see developing in the future?
- What more do you want to learn about career opportunities in this field of work?
- What did you observe that might help you make thoughtful choices about your plans for future careers?

Agencies and Organizations

- What is the purpose of the organization?
- How does it contribute to the life of our community?
- What is the history of the organization: How and why did it get started?
- What kind of organization is it? Nonprofit (independent sector), for-profit (private sector), civic (public sector)?
- How is it funded?
- What programs does it offer?
- Why did it choose to focus on those programs?
- What public policies shape or influence its work?
- How are young people involved in planning or implementing its program?
- How do citizens/volunteers participate in this organization?
- What is its vision for the future?
- How do you think young people could play a larger role in helping this organization?

Connections to Academic Content

- How did you use your academic (math, science, communication) skills in planning or completing this project?

- How did real-world application reinforce and help you build memorable connections for what you are learning in the classroom?

- What did you learn about yourself as a learner? How will you be able to use this insight to help you be a more efficient or effective learner in the future?

- How does the service experience relate to specific class material?

- How did you or adults at your site use writing, reading, communication, science, math, or foreign language skills at your site?

- How did the experience contradict or reinforce the class material?

- How did course material help you overcome obstacles or dilemmas in the service experience?

- What aspects of your learning may have been due to your service?

Social Action and Citizenship

- Why do you think it is important to promote this positive action in the community?

- What compels you to do this work?

- How do you hope youth, families, the elderly, the environment, and the community at large will benefit from this positive action?

- What other initiatives are similar that you can work with or support with your efforts?

- How can it be developed so it builds strong, lasting connections with various members of the community?

- How can you develop it so it's most likely to sustain over time?

- What community need, work challenge, or public issue have you given the most deliberate, critical, or analytical thought to this year? What are some factors and facts you looked at or data you considered? Whom or what resources did you consult?

- Over the next two years, what's one issue or challenge on which you would like to be a more respected authority? How will this be a challenge for you?

Specific Social Issues

- Why is there a need for your service?

- What can you do with the knowledge you gained from the experience to promote change?

- What is the responsibility of a person in this field to address this issue?

- How has your orientation to or opinion about this issue changed through the service-learning experience?

- Why is this issue important to the community?

- How does it impact people in our local or global community?

- Does it impact a large number of people? How do you know that?

- What causes or contributes to this issue?

- Are most people aware of this issue?

- How did you become aware of this issue?

- What is being done to address the issue?

- What could be done to prevent it?

Connections to Service/Empathy

- What is service? What is the difference between service and volunteering?

- Has your definition of service changed? Why? How? Should everyone do service?

- Describe a person you met on your project. What are his/her attitudes about the project? Where might those attitudes have come from?

- What communities or identity groups are you a member of? How might this be related with your commitment to service?

- Have you ever felt hopelessness, despair, discouragement, or burnout related to your service? How have you dealt with this? How can reflection help?

- What are some of the problems facing the world today? How does your service connect to or address these issues?

- Identify a person, group, or community that you got to know this year who is significantly "other" for you. What are the needs or challenges facing them that particularly got to you? What is one way in which you've changed as a result of knowing these folks?

- Dedicating ourselves to service rather than selfishness or our own comfort can be scary. We risk honestly getting to know others who are different, and come face to face, day after day, with pain, abuse, hatred, and violence. What are two fears or inner worries that somehow keep you from being the person of service you hope to become? What is something in your life that brings you courage and gives you hope?

- What is one way in which you expect the community you are serving to nourish, nurture, or satisfy you?

- What are two ways you will take responsibility for that community?

- Summarize the most important things you will take with you from this experience.

- Your commitment to service can involve many things, including keeping your word (also being realistic when you say "yes") and resisting the temptation, at least some of the time, to move on to new causes and needs. Think of something this year that you really didn't want to continue doing, but you kept doing it the best you could. Was there something you got out of that experience?

- What similarities do you perceive between you and the people you are serving?

- How are you perceived by the people you are serving?
- How does their situation impact their life socially, educationally, politically, and recreationally?

Personal Development

- In what ways is your involvement with your service program difficult?
- What personal qualities (e.g., leadership, compassion, speaking) have you developed through service-learning?
- How would you motivate others to become involved in service experiences? What would you say to them?
- What stereotypes are you confronting about the people you serve?
- What new information led you to do this?
- What new things did you learn about your neighborhood or community?
- What people did you meet through the service-learning project? What did you value about their support?

CELEBRATIONS THAT DEMONSTRATE

Now that students have learned something through their experience, they can reach out to other potential community partners—school boards, parent-teacher organizations, media outlets, legislative bodies—to present their findings, share community outcomes, and consider possible next steps. They may do this with a small audience (the leader or the group), or they may demonstrate what they've learned to key community leaders, the media, or a global audience on the Internet. Though demonstration may be part of a grade in a school, the community demonstration provides a powerful opportunity to demonstrate learning in more authentic ways.

DOCUMENTING STUDENT WORK: TELLING THE STORY

Throughout the service-learning project, it is important to "tell the story." If you don't document it, it is as if it never happened.

Why Document?

Telling the story increases the learning. It's like teaching others: it requires the student to become "expert" in the process of the project. Telling the story also increases the service. It can be viewed as a gift of knowledge to the larger community, as the student shares not only what he or she did, but what he or she learned and what others can learn. Telling the story also helps a student relate to (reflect on) the project.

The most important learning outcome of a research project is for a learner to encounter new information and have new experiences, and then to consider them in the light of his or her personal experiences of the world, including intellectual and emotional beliefs about what matters. In other words, to deepen the learners' personal understanding of the world and themselves.

Whom Do You Tell?

Who needs to know about your work? Brainstorm a list that includes people at all levels, from the school/district level and parents to the county, state, and even federal levels.

How Do You Document?

Students can creatively "tell the story" in many ways. Consider:

- A traditional research paper
- A radio show
- A video
- A presentation of evidence or testimony
- Learning festivals that demonstrate how we can help our communities
- A newspaper article
- Public awareness sessions
- Public hearings
- School board presentations
- School TV broadcasts
- School assemblies or advisories
- School fairs
- Community events—conferences, seminars, exhibits
- A dramatic reading
- A photo exhibit
- A blog

CELEBRATIONS IN ACTION

Below are some examples of service-learning project celebrations.

Science Fair Extraordinaire

At Heritage High School, well-dressed fifth graders from three elementary schools filled the gymnasium with their science fair projects. Their high school science coaches were thrilled as they listened to "their students" present the results of their research. Trained high school students, teachers, and district office staff judged the projects, and the room was abuzz while the ribbons were handed out. State and federal legislators and city and county officials meandered through the rows of exhibits, stopping to chat with the elementary and high school students.

Senior Exhibitions That Make a Lasting Difference

Students at Riverdale High School make a full presentation of their Senior Exhibitions to students and faculty, summarizing the year-long research and service-learning work they have done that makes a sustainable impact on the community. Each of these projects is guided by a thought-provoking essential question. Students facilitate a 45-minute discussion of the issue and respond to a string of questions from students. Because they know students and faculty will ask challenging questions, they are thoroughly prepared to demonstrate their mastery of the subject and explain how the service they have done can have a lasting impact on this issue. Then students have a public exhibition to which they invite family and friends to learn about or experience some dimension of the project itself. As they share the important learning that has happened through the project, they also explain their plans for the future—and how those plans have been refined by their project.

Community Speaks Out

Centennial Learning Center Students interviewed Vietnam veterans, people who had chosen to be conscientious objectors to that war, and refugees from African civil wars. Based on the essential questions, "What is the human experience of violence and war? How does war affect humanity?" students interviewed and captured the stories of people whose lives had been affected by wars around the globe. Students recorded their stories, wrote poems and essays in response, and published them all in a book. This book was sold to raise funds for Africa House, a transitional home for African refugees. The demonstration/celebration was held at a public coffee shop. Students invited all the people who had been interviewed, and encouraged them to invite family members. That evening, students read passages from their interviews and some of their own writing, and distributed books to the people they had interviewed. At the close of the evening the students had raised nearly $1,000 for Africa House from the proceeds of their book.

These are just a few examples of demonstrations that are also celebrations. In all instances students are presenting evidence of their intellectual and civic work in a very public and authentic setting. Demonstrations ensure that the work is both seen and heard and that students and the community acknowledge both their thinking and their willingness to take action. These demonstrations can be very public or very personal, simple or an elaborate showcase, student-designed or part of a larger public event. It is important that students have an opportunity to process and think about the work they have done and articulate both their actions and what they have learned from their actions. By demonstrating what they have learned and how what they have learned will affect their personal and civic action, students have the opportunity to synthesize their thinking, and, by sharing it in "public," they are both affirmed by their community and supported in their next steps.

Students can also use these demonstrations as an opportunity to thank all who are involved in the service-learning efforts. This honoring and recognition is not just gracious—it also helps cement the experience in young people's lives.

RESOURCES

The Art of Powerful Questions: Catalyzing Insight, Innovation, and Action by Eric E. Vogt, Juanita Brown, and David Isaacs. Whole Systems Associates: Mill Valley, CA, 2003. At theworldcafe.com/articles/aopq.pdf.

A Practitioner's Guide to Reflection in Service-Learning: Student Voices and Reflection by J. Eyler, D. Giles, and A. Schmiede. Vanderbilt University: Nashville, 2009. The authors explain how and why reflection is important in service-learning, using the words of students themselves, to describe its impacts. They explain different learning styles and give suggestions for matching reflection activities to students' styles. The book also includes numerous ideas for reflection, using the modes of reading, writing, doing, and telling.

Reflection: A Guide to Effective Service-Learning. Sponsored by the National Dropout Prevention Center, this guide offers tools and ideas for creating learning environments and facilitating reflection during each step of a service-learning project. At dropoutprevention.org/publica/servlear_pub/servlear_pub2.htm.

Connecting Thinking and Action: Ideas for Service-Learning Reflection. RMC Research Corporation: Denver, CO, 2003. This guide provides a variety of reflection activities for different subjects and grade levels. Activities are included for each phase of reflection, including the service activity, pre-service, during service, and post-service.

The **Coalition of Essential Schools** has done extensive writing about the attributes of effective exhibitions, and service-learning practitioners can benefit from their resources. Demonstrations are strongest when they show careful selection of topic and format, incorporate required skills and areas of knowledge, involve a variety of human and material resources, and show evidence of reflection and habits of mind. At essentialschools.org.

Note: Some material in this chapter was adapted from "Reflection: Facilitating Learning Connections" by Susan Abravanel, Keisha Edwards, and Kate McPherson, in *Service-Learning: Building School-Community Partnerships to Support Career-Related Learning and Extended Application Standards*: Portland, OR, 2006, and from © 2004 The Montana Heritage Project at www.edheritage.org.

Building and Sustaining Service-Learning Programs

This section contains material adapted from the Maryland State Department of Education, and from the Project Service Leadership website. Used with permission. At mssa.sailorsite .net/middle_school_guide.pdf and projectserviceleadership.org

No matter how dedicated you are, your service class or club will be much more successful if you garner support in the school and community at large. It's also a comfort to have friends with whom you can commiserate. Think about ways to approach the principal or program administrators, fellow staff, parents, community, and press. The following are a few strategies to consider in building support for your program.

SCHOOL PRINCIPAL OR PROGRAM ADMINISTRATOR

A key factor in initiating and sustaining student service-learning in your school or program is determining the best strategy for gaining support. The obvious place to begin is with the principal or program administrator. You need her or his support, but what is the best way to gain it?

Ask yourself: Is this an administrator who wants to know everything (i.e., no action without prior approval)? Is he or she someone who would prefer to be approached with a well-developed plan? Would your principal or administrator prefer students to be part of the initial approach? If so, get the students excited and have them approach him or her with their ideas.

Essentially, figure out the preferences of your principal or administrator and pitch your plea for support accordingly. Consider yourself and your students marketers:

before you can successfully sell your idea, you must analyze your consumer's needs and interests.

What interests your principal or administrator the most? Some want value-improved test scores the most, while others want a motivated student body, pleased parents, students taking charge, positive community relations, or strengthening the school or program's reputation as an innovator.

Once you feel comfortable with approaching your principal or administrator, prepare your plan of action:

1. Set up a time for an appointment, and make sure it is long enough to discuss issues.

2. Prepare yourself. Ask yourself why you want to get involved and what you think would be advantages to the project, as well as any pitfalls you anticipate and how to overcome them. Write out important points and practice your presentation. In addition, make sure no other faculty member is already doing this. If someone is already spearheading a movement toward service-learning, offer to join forces.

3. Go in with a specific service project, with details worked out—regardless of whether or not you believe your principal or administrator will want to hear them at this time. Choose a project that includes only your class, and don't expect other teachers or program workers to be involved until you demonstrate success. Most people are advised to "start small," but there are exceptions to this rule: it could be a good idea to do a school- or program-wide service day that would coincide with other activities around the state. (Note: If you decide to do this, provide a number of choices to everyone about ways they can get involved. People like to feel that they have options and can be creative if they desire.)

4. Clarify in your own mind what you aim to accomplish.

5. Be open to suggestions from the principal or administrator. Ask questions so he or she can provide some input.

6. As you implement the project, provide written updates to your principal or administrator, to faculty or program staff, and to parents. Spread as much credit to other people as you can.

FELLOW TEACHERS OR PROGRAM STAFF

Inform others about your plans for service-learning. It is much better to talk to people individually rather than as a group, so that they feel singled out and appreciated. Let them know what is going on, particularly if they are involved in service themselves.

If you can, try to involve other teachers or staff in a service project. Form a committee to pull together different service activities to generate excitement for service and create the peer support you need to keep your own spirits up. The group should try to meet on a regular basis.

Another way to get teachers or program staff excited is to have the students approach them. Have students go to each class or group and make a presentation about service. They should use creative approaches—a rap, song, poem, skit, commercial, or game show theme—that is no longer than three minutes. Ask the students to survey teachers or program staff to discover what they care about, so the students can help.

SUPPORT STAFF

Remember the support staff! Involve them in the activities—or make one of your first service projects a "Staff Appreciation Day." Remember to include the custodians and the building and grounds staff. They can provide crucial support for beautification projects and recycling efforts.

PARENTS

Many parents can recognize the value of service-learning that others do not see—but it's up to you and your students to get them involved. Inform parents of the philosophy, goals, and activities of your service-learning program. Invite them to work with students. They could help teach service-learning materials or accompany students to a service site.

The actual experience of helping another person can turn even the biggest doubters around. At one school, a parent vigorously objected to her child visiting a homeless shelter, stating that such an activity was not educationally sound and might give her child nightmares. However, she agreed to accompany her child to the shelter. Upon arriving, one of the homeless children ran up to her and gave her an enormous hug. She never objected again. One service engagement is usually worth a thousand arguments.

Keep in mind that most parents work. Think of ways they can participate without having to rearrange their schedules. To get you started, here are some ideas for encouraging parental involvement:

- Inform parents of service plans. Send parents a letter describing your plans and suggesting ways they can help. Update them on projects by sending them samples of students' work, such as something from a reflection activity (creative writing or art) to illustrate how students feel about serving.

- Talk about caring. Following a discussion on what they care about in their community, have students ask a parent or family member, "What do you care about in our community?" Students can report on what they discover.

- How have our families served others? Ask students to compile a family and neighborhood history. They can work with their parents to answer: "How have members of our family helped others?" Each student can document his or her information on a page of a class book.

- Identify community needs and resources. Have students ask parents for suggestions regarding where they should serve in their community. If you need extra library books about a certain topic, see if parents will help obtain them.

- Have students give presentations to PTA meetings and other parent organizations.

SUSTAINING YOUR PERSONAL PRACTICE

In most schools and community programs it is possible to implement service-learning year after year if students are doing well academically. Most service-learning program examples in this book are led by teachers and youth workers who have championed their own programs and frequently played a leadership role in their school or community.

"Some of the students I had when they were 12 and 13 are now 20 or even 30. I get to hear time after time, 'That community experience stuck with me. It had a powerful impact on me and the choices I made for my career. Thank you.'"

"I see too many students turned off to school because they are not inspired. Service-learning helps them see they have gifts and strengths and talents for the world, and we need them. I live and work in a valuable resource—the Puget Sound—that is in trouble. We need their young creative ideas."

"Too many students lose their wonder and passion. Service-learning has been the one way I have seen that keeps that fire alive."

"I sustain myself by connecting my passions to my work. If my students see that I don't care much about the work that I'm doing, then they won't connect with it either. I do not want my students to think that their education is just another hoop to jump through to get them to graduation. Rather, I allow students to use their voice and choice within their education and this, in turn, allows them to participate in service that connects with their own interests and curiosity to the world around them. When that choice is allowed, the ownership, quality, and depth of their learning sustains me."

"They use journals to write about their experience. When I am really pulling my hair out I think about what they have written and I think, 'Oh, come on, we can do this. It's about the kids.'"

"I love to watch children come alive as they make something happen in their world. That sets me on fire. It makes my heart sing!"

"This kind of teaching is hopeful but not naïve, because it is likely to produce well-educated young people prepared to fight for a more just world."

Embedded within each of these statements are some easy ways for educators to take steps that will help sustain our work over time.

- If teachers and program workers value reading or hearing student testimonials, keeping a few notes or photos handy will reconnect you with the value of their work, even when the going gets tough.
- If engaging adults and youth will help community or environmental issues that are important to you, create a chart or photo that illustrates the impact of their efforts over time.

- If you're serious about improving your practice, become part of a network of teachers or youth workers who teach similar content and make a commitment to visit each other's classrooms to provide coaching.

- If you enjoy learning about the long-term impact your program has on your students, don't assume you will hear from alumni. Build an alumni survey or organize a retrospective study. One teacher just did a 10-year retrospective of one of her programs and was amazed to hear what her former students had to say. In addition, it was great data to support her current grant applications.

- If you need to take care of yourself by building in rigorous exercise or a nap, recruit colleagues to hold you accountable.

CONFERENCES AND INSTITUTES

Service-learning leaders regularly say that attending conferences helps them learn from other teachers and program workers, and, even more important, makes them feel like they are part of a community of people who care deeply about the practice of service-learning and know its value and challenges.

The **National Service-Learning Conference** is held each spring in different locations across the country. This is the largest conference that focuses on school-based service-learning, and it is a great opportunity to bring teachers, board members, students, and community partners together to hear about effective practice. Find out more at nylc.org.

The **Powerful Personal Projects Summer Institute** meets every summer in Portland, OR. Enrollment is open to those who provide leadership for culminating projects. Find out more at projectserviceleadership.org.

The **Urban Institute,** sponsored by the National Youth Leadership Council, is held each summer for teachers and youth workers who work in urban settings. Learn more at nylc.org.

The **BigTent Conference,** hosted by Search Institute, is held every November in partnership with a variety of organizations. Find out more at BigTent.org.

For other service-learning institutes, check out the National Service Learning Clearinghouse at servicelearning.org.

SELF-RENEWAL RESOURCES

The **Center for Courage & Renewal** helps foster personal and professional renewal through supporting retreats that offer the time and space to slow down and reflect on life and work. These retreats—based in the Circle of Trust® approach—are often called Courage to Teach® or Courage to Lead®, are led by skilled facilitators, and make use of poetry and stories, solitude, reflection, and deep listening. At couragerenewal.org.

Putting More Joy in Your Job, by Kate McPherson, is a practical guide for professional renewal that helps educators increase their experience of job satisfaction and resolve sources of dissatisfaction. Order at projectserviceleadership.org.

How Was Your *Day at School? Improving Dialogue about Teacher Job Satisfaction* by Nathan Eklund, Minneapolis: Search Institute, 2009. This book contains advice and practical strategies for avoiding teacher burnout and discussion questions to enhance the teacher-administrator relationship.

Sustaining the Soul that Serves provides educational programs for service leaders that help sustain them in their work for social justice and peace. At sustainingthesoulthatserves.org.

PROFESSIONAL DEVELOPMENT RESOURCES

Professional Learning in the Learning Professional: A Status Report on Teacher Development in the United States and Abroad by L. Darling-Hammond, R. C. Wei, A. Andree, N. M. Richardson, and S. Orphanos. Stanford University Press, 2009. This report is part of a multi-year research effort to identify the forms of professional learning that improve practice and student learning. Downloadable at nsdc.org.

The **Service-Learning Providers Network** contains a resource library, interest groups, personal profiles, and much more. At slprovidersnetwork.org.

The **National Staff Development Council** is the largest nonprofit professional association committed to ensuring success for all students through staff development and school improvement. At nsdc.org.

The **Generator School Network** is a community that links educators who are passionate about service-learning. At gsn.nylc.org.

The **School Reform Initiative** provides Professional Learning Communities training and resources. At schoolreforminitiative.org

The National Youth Leadership Council (nylc.org) and Portland State University (ceed .pdx.edu/service-learning) both provide **online teacher service-learning certification programs**.

INDEX

academic content, connections to, 104
academic environment, 18
academic need, 25
academic skills, 23
academic standards, 95
adult partners, preparing, 77
agencies, 103
   learning about, 54
assessment, 74
   evidence, 97
   process, 92–93
   strategies, 90–92
assumptions inventory, 100

background checks, 82
budget, creating, 83

careers, 103
celebrations, 20, 106–108
citizenship, 104
civic
   education, 65
   engagement, 70
   knowledge, 70
   literacy, 65
   skills, 85
civic responsibility meter, 70–71
communication skills, 70
community impact, 85
community mapping, 100
community members, interviewing, 44

community needs
   identifying, 40
   transforming into projects, 45, 46
community organizations, 42
   choosing, 37–39
community ownership, 20
community partners
   cultural, 63
   reaching out to, 53
community problem, 24, 26, 29
conferences, 115
culturally responsive teaching, 60
curriculum
   formal, 67
   focus, 24
   link to, 14, 56
cycle of service learning, 18–21

discussion questions, 103
diversity, 15, 57, 61–63
documenting work, 106–107
dropout rates, 52
duration, 18

empowerment, 56
evaluation, 20, 21, 86
experience, meaningful, 20, 51–52

goals
   learning, 97
   program, 74
   student learning, 23, 91
government, 66

history, 66

idea generation, 32, 73
implementation, 86

journals, 102, 105

know-want-learn chart, 100
knowledge inventory, 100

law, 66
leadership, 55
learning
   emphases, 33
   objectives, 21
   evidence of, 88, 90, 97
liability, 78

materials, 86
   gathering, 83
meaningful service, 14
medical care, 80

needs, genuine, 18, 20

observation, 20
organizations, 103
   helping, 24, 26
   learning about, 54
   youth-serving, 29–30
orientation
   parent, 79
   planning, 83

student, 79
teacher/supervisor, 81
to work, 75
ownership, 21, 86

parents, 113
engaging, 75
partners, 41
engaging, 83
partnerships, 16–17
establishing, 38
performance creation, 24, 25–26, 29
personal development, 106
personal practice, 114–115
personal value, fostering, 52
philanthropic venture, 24, 27
plan, develop and outline, 74
planning tool, 85
planning, 21, 73
guidelines, 79
logistical, 83
problem-solving skills, 70
product creation, 24, 25, 29
progress monitoring, 17
Project Citizen, 66
public meeting, 44
public policy, influence, 26–27
publicity plan, 83

quality practice, 74
questions
for students, 49
for teachers, 45

reflection, 15, 86
post-service, 101
pre-service, 99, 100
relationships, building, 52
research study, 24, 25–26
resources, 22, 30–31, 47, 57, 64, 69,
82, 86, 96, 108–109
financial, 75
gathering, 74
logistical, 75
people, 75
potential, 41
professional development, 116
self-renewal, 116
roles, 84
defining, 74

safeguards, 78
safety, 80, 83
service site, 81
service types, benefits and
challenges of, 34–35
service-learning standards, 13

service
connections to, 105
meaningful, 21
skills
building, 76
career-related, 85
life, 85
social action, 104
social issues, 104
standards, 85
of practice, 61
reviewing, 74
students, engaging, 20, 53
success, 73, 102
supervision, 80
support staff, 113
sustaining service learning, 111

teach others, 24, 25
transportation, 83

youth involvement, continuum of,
55
youth voice, 16, 51, 55

About the Author

Kate McPherson, M.A.T., is the director of Project Service Leadership. For over 25 years she has provided professional development and consultation on service-learning with K–12 schools and districts, colleges of educations, youth development organizations, nonprofit organizations, and K–20 service-learning collaboratives. She teaches online courses for the service-learning certificate program for Portland State University's Graduate School of Education. She has also written service-learning curricula for universities, school districts, faith-based organizations, and youth development organizations.

Kate's publications include *Enriching the Curriculum through Service-Learning, Discover Contextual Teaching and Learning—Service-Learning, Getting to the Heart of School Renewal: A Principal's Guide for Implementing Thoughtful Service-Learning Programs and Policies, Education and Urban Society,* and *A Parent's Guide to Family Service.* Kate has also written service-learning resources for the Washington State Principals' Associations.

She has served on Washington State's Commission for National and Community Service and on the advisory board for Facing the Future, Generator School Network, and the Giraffe Project. She is currently forming a regional and national network to support schools and districts that are committed to engaging all high school seniors in rigorous and meaningful culminating projects.

She currently lives in Vancouver, Washington, with her husband, Brad, and her daughter Elin.

more great books

FROM SEARCH INSTITUTE PRESS

www.search-institute.org

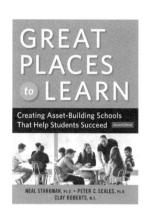

GREAT PLACES TO LEARN
by Neal Starkman, Ph.D., Peter C. Scales, Ph.D., and Clay Roberts, M.S.

How to create a school environment where students will thrive.
Research shows that the Developmental Assets® help students K–12 do well in school and become healthy, caring, responsible members of society. This book includes a clear introduction to the assets, practical ideas for integrating assets throughout your school (no need to start a new program), and firsthand accounts from schools across the country. Inspiring, optimistic, and concrete.

Softcover, 216 pages, CD-ROM of reproducible handouts and tools, $34.95.

ENGAGE EVERY PARENT
by Nancy Tellett-Royce and Susan Wootten

Proven ways to get parents involved in their kids' education and extracurriculars.
Connect with families and encourage parents to sign on, show up, and make a difference. This book covers every step in building good working relationships with parents, from first contact to thanking volunteers. Learn to communicate, plan conferences, make an impact on hard-to-reach parents, even deal with overzealous "helicopter parents."

Softcover, 132 pages, CD-ROM of reproducible handouts, $29.95

TRAINING PEER HELPERS
by Barbara B. Varenhorst, Ph.D.

Teach kids to help each other through problems and tough times.
Give kids the tools they need to help each other. Fifteen 90-minute sessions teach communication, assertiveness, confidentiality, decision-making, and conflict resolution skills. Kids learn to be good observers, ask questions, listen, resist negative peer pressure, and more.

Softcover, 176 pages, CD-ROM of reproducible handouts, $35.95

PARENT, TEACHER, MENTOR, FRIEND
by Peter L. Benson, Ph.D., president of Search Institute

Simple, everyday ways to build positive relationships with young people.
Every young person needs positive relationships with adults. A nationally recognized expert in child and teen development, Benson describes simple ways to reach out to kids. (*Examples:* Use 30-second encounters to offer compliments and recognition. Ask meaningful questions that lead to deeper conversation. Learn what matters most to kids.) He shares real-life stories of efforts that have had lasting significance, and he invites every adult to step up.

Softcover, 204 pages, $7.95

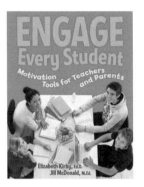

ENGAGE EVERY STUDENT
by Elizabeth Kirby, Ed.D., and Jill McDonald, M.Ed.

Dozens of ready-to-use tools give kids the desire and the confidence to learn.
Help kids really want to learn with handouts, activities, and best-practice tips designed to get them excited and keep them connected. Learn why some kids lack motivation, and tailor learning activities accordingly. Create a positive parent-teacher-student relationship that will encourage learning both in and out of the classroom. Incorporates the Developmental Assets.

Softcover, 128 pages; reproducible handouts, $21.95

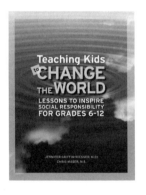

TEACHING KIDS TO CHANGE THE WORLD
by Jennifer Griffin-Wiesner, M.Ed., and Chris Maser, M.S.

Twenty-six easy-to-use lessons inspire social consciousness and action. Kids learn to think critically and view the world through their strengths.

Softcover, 104 pages, reproducible handouts, $19.95

MAKE A WORLD OF DIFFERENCE
by Dawn C. Oparah

Fifty asset-building activities help teens explore diversity, become more culturally aware, examine their own attitudes and behaviors, and build relationships.

Softcover, 112 pages, reproducible handouts, $26.95